What Others Are Saying about

TO EACH IS GIVEN

To Each is Given is marked by biblical conviction, detailed clarity and humble courage. I found my understanding of spiritual gifts confirmed in some areas and challenged in others. Read Timothy Clothier's book. Read it with an open Bible, an open heart, and an open mind.

> **Larry E. McCall**, D. Min. Author of *Walking Like Jesus Did,*
> *Loving Your Wife as Christ Loves the Church*, and *Grandparenting*
> *with Grace*
> Warsaw, Ind.

Timothy Clothier sets forth the biblical and theological reasoning upon which he has constructed his view of the role of spiritual gifts, signs, and wonders in the church today. His gracious tone models how to respond with respect and conviction to Christians holding opposing views on this issue, particularly charismatics and the New Apostolic Reformation. Even more, his careful and thorough approach to Scripture, and his desire to allow Scripture to speak for itself, provide a valuable resource for everyone who desires greater clarity on how the Holy Spirit does – and does not – continue working among us today.

> **Adam Copenhaver**, PhD in New Testament, ThM in Old
> Testament, pastor, Grace Brethren Church
> Mabton, Wash.

Though this topic often solicits intense reaction without listening and resorting to preconceived theological conclusions, Clothier shines exegetical light on the pertinent biblical passages to help us take a deep dive into the world of the first-century world where Paul (and Peter) were addressing these same disruptive problems. Without name calling, he sets the pace for how we can allow the New Testament to inform our understanding of spiritual gifts in our churches today. There's plenty of room for more dialogue, but this book gives us plenty to talk about and even more to agree about as we take Scripture seriously and unity just as seriously.

Jeremy Wike, senior pastor, Community of Hope Church
Columbia City, Ind.

In *To Each Is Given*, Clothier blends biblical precision with pastoral care as he revisits the complicated topic of spiritual gifts. He systematically works through relevant texts of Scripture, defining key words, analyzing commentaries, and providing personal insights. Clothier gracefully touches on gender roles and thoughtfully challenges modern abuses of "signs and wonders." His respect for God's Word, the Spirit's power, and church's unity resonate throughout this book.

Tim Sprankle, pastor, Grace Church and doctoral student at
Biola University
Leesburg, Ind.

Born out of deep pastoral concern, and an equally deep love for the truths of the Word of God, Timothy Clothier charts out a via media on the issue of spiritual gifts in *To Each Is Given*. Not landing in the traditional charismatic or cessationist camps, he thoughtfully exegetes the Word of God to examine the questions of which spiritual gifts are active today, and how we utilize them for the glory of God and the building up of the Body of Christ. As the number of pastor-theologians seem sadly to be ebbing away, Timothy reminds us that there is no substitute for having a firm grasp on the eternal truths of the inerrant Word of God as we seek to shepherd and lead the Church as we are called.

Davey Ermold, Th.M, pastor, Blue Ridge Grace Brethren
Church
Winchester, Va.

Taking complicated subject matters and making them understandable is a 'gift' that Timothy leverages throughout *To Each is Given*. I believe this will be a tremendous tool on the bookshelves of pastors who desire to teach a Biblical perspective of spiritual gifts in our modern context. Whether you're looking for sermon prep material or your next small group study, *To Each is Given* is a must have!

Mark Lingenfelter, president of Inspire: Charis Fellowship Pastors Network and pastor, Grace Fellowship Church Duncansville, Pa.

TO EACH IS GIVEN

Spiritual Gifts in
The Life of The Church

TO EACH IS GIVEN

Spiritual Gifts in The Life of The Church

TIMOTHY CLOTHIER

P.O. Box 544
Winona Lake, IN 46590
bmhbooks.com
800-348-2756

To Each Is Given
Spiritual Gifts in the Life of the Church

Copyright © 2020 by Timothy Clothier

ISBN 978-0-88469-361-1 (print)
   978-0-88469-362-8 (ebook)
REL062000 RELIGION / Spirituality
REL067000 RELIGION / Christian Theology / General
REL099000 RELIGION / Christian Living / Spiritual Warfare

Published by BMH Books
Box 544, Winona Lake, Ind.
bmhbooks.com

Printed in the United States of America

Cover and interior design: Terry Julien

DEDICATION

TO MY FATHER,
DR. THOMAS CLOTHIER

You are the greatest theologian
I know because you live out
what you believe. Your faithful
preaching, teaching, and parenting
have done more to shape my
theology and hermeneutic than all
my schooling has. Your steadfast
living continually serves as an
active testimony of the Bible's
unwavering truthfulness and
God's unending faithfulness.

AND TO MY WIFE,
CARRIE CLOTHIER

Words are unable to fully express
my love and appreciation. Your
constant support, listening ear,
critical thinking, and desire to
glorify Jesus have made this
project a reality. I love you.

TABLE OF CONTENTS

Introduction

I remember the day like it was yesterday. My wife Carrie and I were living in Indiana at the time, and on this evening, we were playing Ticket to Ride in our living room. We were alone, having just put our daughter Allegra to bed, when we heard a knock at the door. Stopping by was one of our close friends, Susan. We knew Susan well and had spent a considerable amount of time with her over the years.

We first met Susan in 2006. She was one of the 30 students on a summer ministry team that Carrie and I led. That fall Susan moved to Indiana to take classes at Grace College, and while doing so she attended our church.

For two summers, during her time at Grace, Susan lived with us and became known as Aunt Susan to our daughter. She was one of many college students in our lives whom we grew to love deeply.

That night, Susan had some big news to share with us. She was leaving Indiana and enrolling in the Bethel School of Supernatural Ministry (BSSM). I was floored, bewildered, speechless, shocked, angry, concerned, and hurt.

Up to this point, Susan had sought counsel from my wife and me for many of the major life decisions she had made during college. Yet, here was a blockbuster of a decision that was made without any advice from us, or even an advanced warning.[1] Her decision had already been made, and she was stopping by to simply inform us of it.

During the previous year, I had become vaguely familiar with BSSM through another mutual friend whose son was enrolled in the

---

1 To be clear, I am not asserting that all my emotions that night and the rationale behind them were proper or right.

program at the time. She and her husband were very involved in our local church. However, her son was not, having been away at college for four years. Consequently, many of the discussions about BSSM and her son didn't lead to the same set of emotions because I didn't know him nearly as well.

Nevertheless, there we sat in our living room trying to make sense out of what Susan had just told us. More than anything I felt troubled by what we had just heard and what I believed Susan was getting herself into. Immediately after she left, I jumped on the internet and began searching for BSSM, eager to learn and understand just what kind of school this was. In many ways, what I found confirmed my fears.

That evening began what I have since referred to as the most difficult season of ministry I have ever been through. I felt like I was flung headlong into a theological rabbit hole, trying to understand and unpack the beliefs of BSSM and the New Apostolic Reformation (NAR). This hole seemingly had no bottom and, over several years, I had my theological convictions deeply challenged, resulting in both confirmation and change.

About two and a half years after that initial conversation, I began to sense that I was crawling out of the hole. Susan was nearing the end of her three-year program with BSSM and, in many ways, I was nearing the end of a similar three-year program with not just a greater understanding of BSSM and the NAR, but of the Bible and what God reveals about spiritual gifts.

This book aims to articulate what I learned throughout that two-and-a-half-year journey and what I have learned since. At the beginning of this journey, I would have espoused cessationist positions and arguments; however, this is not the case any longer. I am now positionally a continuationist.

As a continuationist, I believe that the entire list of spiritual gifts, outlined in several different passages, is still operational for the church today. Furthermore, I believe that the church desperately needs all these gifts. However, I must still reject the claims of the NAR and

BSSM, among others, that signs and wonders are for today and that believers should chase them.

I am also more confident than ever that the local church and her leaders must think carefully before allowing the resources and influences of the NAR into their midst. The signs and wonders theology and teaching of the NAR is dangerous and should be avoided.

At times I will specifically reference or quote a teaching or teacher within the NAR. However, more than anything I desire that this book clearly communicates what I am for, not merely what I am against. Throughout the following pages I intend to contend for what I understand the Bible to teach about spiritual gifts, signs and wonders, and how each has their place in God's redemptive plan.

I am convinced that signs and wonders are not for the church today, and the church should not be chasing them. However, it is also my conviction that signs and wonders are not the same as spiritual gifts. In fact, much of the difficulty surrounding spiritual gifts in the church today may be due to lack of differentiation between signs and wonders and spiritual gifts. Such differentiation is needed as local churches seek to be Spirit-filled congregations who glorify Christ, make disciples, and serve with all the gifts that the Holy Spirit has given them.

In Part I, we will consider whether spiritual gifts are the same as signs and wonders. Both appear in the Scriptures and have similarities between them, but we must not assume that they are the same.

In Part II, we will turn our attention to the spiritual gifts found in the New Testament and look at a definition for each. Specifically, we will do so considering how each gift fits into the body metaphor and how each gift might be utilized today.

Before we begin, I feel compelled to briefly answer the most common questions or objections that might be raised by those who will pick up this book. I also want to outline the boundary lines and clearly communicate what I am not saying before I seek to communicate what I am saying. While not an exhaustive list, here are some of the most common questions or objections that I personally have found myself asking when interacting with this subject.

TO EACH IS GIVEN

Does any spiritual gift or experience have a higher authority than the Word of God?

Absolutely not! God's Word is our highest authority, and any gift or experience that contradicts God's Word is to be dismissed.

Is God still revealing new Scripture today?

Absolutely not! I believe that the 66 books of the Old and New Testaments are the inspired, infallible, Word of God and what God has specially revealed to us.

Are there Apostles/apostles or Prophets/prophets in the church today?

Absolutely not! To help provide clarity throughout this book and distinguish between the disciples whom Jesus made Apostles and others who may be authorized messengers that are sent out, I will capitalize the word Apostle when referring to the original twelve and lowercase apostle when referring to those not in the original group, save Paul.[2] Because of Judas's commissioning and subsequent betrayal, it is not helpful to use the words original twelve to create such a distinction. Furthermore, Paul's addition to the group of Apostles also leaves the words original twelve unhelpful since he was added later as one "untimely born." Equally, I will capitalize the word Prophet when referring to the Old Testament Prophets.

Where are all the stories?

Throughout the book, you may find yourself wondering why there are not more stories and personal testimonies to support the conclusions I am contending for. While this is a fair question, I have intentionally not wanted my arguments to be supported by stories and personal testimonies. I have done this specifically with both my cessationist and charismatic friends in mind.

To my charismatic friends, I ask you to step away from your stories and consider anew what God's Word says about signs and wonders and spiritual gifts. We have something more sure than even the

---

2 The exception will be when I am providing a direct quotation or a source that does not capitalize the word.

greatest spiritual experiences, the Word of God (2 Peter 1:19). God has spoken, and it is in our best interest to draw near and listen. Only from this conviction are we then able to interpret what we experience.

To my cessationist friends, I know that personal testimonies and stories will not convince you! For that I am glad, and here we completely agree. Consequently, there are few stories in this book because my desire is to put forth a compelling biblical argument for you to consider.

Where is the test?

A quick Google search will invariably lead you to dozens of spiritual gift tests. I remember being given such tests in high school and college and giving such tests when I worked with teens and young adults. In and of themselves, these tests are not bad or wrong, though I personally have come to find them unhelpful. Consequently, there is no test included in this book.

In discerning your spiritual gift(s) I believe it is more beneficial to ask three specific questions than it is to take a test. (1) What are you passionate about? (2) How has God used you in the past/where do you see the most fruit? (3) What do those closest to you think your spiritual gifts are?

Is this book intended to be the definitive work on spiritual gifts, and will all questions be answered?

By no means. I seek to plow a new middle road between the New Apostolic Reformation/hyper-charismatic churches and cessationist groups by exposing the danger of the NAR while encouraging cessationists to consider again whether spiritual gifts have ceased or not. Invariably, some questions will be left unanswered.

Furthermore, and in full disclosure, I am well aware that arguments will be made that each side will find unsatisfying and lacking. Nevertheless, there is real spiritual danger within the NAR movement; and we need to be vigilant regarding it. Also, we must not err in denying the spiritual gifts that have been given by God to the church.

For the glory and fame of Jesus, to each has been given.
Timothy Clothier

PART I

Signs and Wonders, and Spiritual Gifts

1

DEFINING
THEOLOGICAL CAMPS

Across the church today a wide range of convictions and definitions exist regarding spiritual gifts. These theological positions range between the belief that some spiritual gifts ceased in the first or second century, to the belief that believers in the church can operate with the same level of giftedness and authority as the Apostles did. Unfortunately, what does not exist today, to my knowledge, is a consistent and agreed-upon set of definitions that explain what spiritual gifts are and what they are not. Nor is there a mutual understanding of how signs and wonders fit into the discussion of spiritual gifts.

Many seem to simply assume that signs and wonders are spiritual gifts and vice versa. In this book, we will seek to define what signs and wonders are, what spiritual gifts are, consider how they relate to one another, and whether each is for the church today.

Some groups proudly claim signs and wonders are for the church today and happen in their midst—specifically teaching that they be chased. Bob Smietana of *Christianity Today* writes, "Largely behind the scenes, a group of mostly self-proclaimed 'apostles,' leading ministries from North Carolina to Southern California, has [sic] attracted millions of followers with promises of direct access to God through signs and wonders."[1] Danny Silk of Bethel Church and BSSM in Red-

---

1 Bob Smietana, "The 'Prophets' and 'Apostles' Leading the Quiet Revolution in American Religion," *Christianity Today*, August 3, 2017 https://www.christianityto-day.com/ct/2017/august-web-only/bethel-church-international-house-prayer-proph-ets-apostles.html.

ding, California, writes, "sustaining a supernatural lifestyle, where signs and wonders follow us, is therefore totally dependent on living out our true identities as sons and daughters of God."[2] In his book, *Culture of Honor*, Silk seeks to give instructions for how one can live this *supernatural lifestyle*. On the other side of the theological spectrum are those who largely ignore the supernatural work of the Holy Spirit in the lives of believers today.

Personally, I am a part of a fellowship of churches that has unfortunately been known to be guilty of such an error.[3] While I was a student at Grace College and Theological Seminary, we often joked that *our* holy Trinity was the Father, Son, and the Holy Bible! Now, to be clear, no one at Grace was denying the personhood or deity of the Holy Spirit, but many were uncomfortable with His work and were not sure what to do with His filling and glorifying work.[4]

In response to a functional absence of the Holy Spirit in preaching and teaching, a group of individuals emerged who swung the pendulum too far the other way. If one side of this conversation has "ignored the Spirit because we have the Word" the other side has run dangerously close to "ignoring the Word because we have the Spirit." In addition, some of Christianity's most popular songs and books have been written by authors and composers who practice and believe the Holy Spirit still operates through signs and wonders and that the church must continue to pursue these.

In observing how we arrived here, those on the more emotional side of the conversation are absolutely right in desiring more from God than what felt like cold and lifeless doctrine. And those, like myself, prone to cold and lifeless doctrine, have found ourselves challenged to rethink theological positions we believed had long been settled. How-

---

2 Danny Silk, *Culture of Honor.* (Shippensburg: Destiny Image, 2009) Loc. 214 of 2771 Kindle.

3 I am not speaking of the Charis Fellowship in its entirety, since I was not in a position to observe the entire fellowship. I am merely commenting on my experience within the Fellowship as it began at Grace College in 2002 and has continued with pastoral ministry.

4 Acts 2:4 (filling) John 16:14 (glorifying).

ever, neither side has the language with which to speak to the other and, as is often the case, when we disagree and don't know how to speak to one another, we end up shouting and only losing our voices.

To navigate a way forward, we must first begin with definitions of the major positions within this discussion, as well as the words *sign(s), wonders,* and *signs and wonders.* Perhaps defining these terms will provide our churches with the language we need to have profitable, loving, and Christ-glorifying conversations about the role of the Holy Spirit and spiritual gifts in the church today. [5]

Cessationist—"One who believes that certain miraculous spiritual gifts ceased when the apostles died and Scripture was complete."[6]

Continuationist—Within the continuationist camp considerable nuances exist, as the multiple definitions demonstrate:

• "Continuationism is the belief that the supernatural gifts of the Holy Spirit taught in the Bible—such as prophecy, tongues, interpretation of tongues, healings, and miracles—have not ceased and are available for the believer today. Continuationism is the opposite of cessationism which teaches that supernatural gifts have ceased either when the canon of Scripture was completed or at the death of the last apostle."[7]

• "Supernatural gifts are given to every generation and should be practiced today but always tested according to the guidelines of Scripture." [8]

---

5 See Figure 1.1, at the end of this chapter, for a graphic of these positions placed on a continuum. It is interesting to note that many believers and churches today use the term *charismatic* to describe themselves positionally. However, there exists quite a broad range of theological belief under this heading. For example, "Reformed Charismatics" would vary widely from "Pentecostal Charismatics," yet both would claim to be charismatic.

6 Wayne Grudem, *Systematic Theology* (Grand Rapids: Zondervan Publishing, 1994), 1237.

7 Tim Challies, "Why I Am Not Continuationist," at challies.com, July 7, 2016, https://www.challies.com/articles/why-i-am-not-continuationist/.

8 Mark Driscoll, *Doctrine: What Christians Should Believe* (Wheaton: Crossway, 2010), 386.

To Each Is Given

- "Continuationism is the belief that all the spiritual gifts, including healings, tongues, and miracles, are still in operation today, just as they were in the days of the early church. A continuationist believes that the spiritual gifts have 'continued' unabated since the day of Pentecost and that the demonstration of 'signs, wonders, and miracles' (2 Cor. 12:12), as witnessed in the apostolic era, should be a hallmark of today's church as well."[9]

- In slight variation to these definitions, my working definition of continuationism is the belief that the spiritual gifts listed in Romans 12:3–8, 1 Corinthians 12:1–11, Ephesians 4:11 (gifts, not offices), and 1 Peter 4:10 are all supernatural and still in operation today. These spiritual gifts are not to be confused with signs and wonders which ceased with the Apostles.

Charismatic—"A term referring to any groups or people that trace their historical origin to the charismatic renewal movement of the 1960s and 1970s. Such groups seek to practice all the spiritual gifts mentioned in the New Testament, but unlike many Pentecostal denominations, allow differing viewpoints on whether baptism in the Holy Spirit is subsequent to conversion and whether tongues is a sign of baptism in the Holy Spirit."[10]

Pentecostal—"Any denomination or group that traces its historical origin to the Pentecostal revival that began in the United States in 1901 and that holds to the doctrinal positions (a) that baptism in the Holy Spirit is ordinarily an event subsequent to conversion, (b) that baptism in the Holy Spirit is made evident by the sign of speaking in tongues, and (c) that all the spiritual gifts mentioned in the New Testament are to be sought and used today."[11]

New Apostolic Reformation (NAR)—Peter Wagner, who is credited with coining the term New Apostolic Reformation, defines this movement in his book *Apostles and Prophets*.

---

9 "What is Continuationism?" Got Questions, n.d., https://www.gotquestions.org/continuationism.html.

10 Grudem, *Systematic Theology*, 1237–1238.

11 Ibid., 1251.

The New Apostolic Reformation is an extraordinary work of God at the close of the twentieth century which is, to a significant extent, changing the shape of Protestant Christianity around the world ... Particularly in the 1990s, but with roots going back for almost a century, new forms and operational procedures are now emerging in areas such as local church government, interchurch relationships, financing, evangelism, missions, prayer, leadership selection and training, the role of supernatural power, worship and other important aspects of church life. Some of these changes are being seen within denominations themselves, but for the most part they are taking the form of loosely structured apostolic networks.[12]

Hyper-Charismatic or Charismania[13]—The conviction of churches/movements largely focused on signs and wonders. Claims of glory clouds of gold dust, guaranteed healing,[14] angel feathers,[15] fire tunnels,[16] diamonds appearing in sanctuaries,[17] being slain in the spirit,[18] etc., are made by proponents of this theological position. Further-

12 C. Peter Wagner. *Apostles and Prophets: The Foundation of the Church* (Minneapolis: Chosen, 2000), 21. Wagner acknowledges on pg. 114 that he was one of the initial individuals doing research on the NAR and hints that he created the term.

13 The term *charismania* is not likely to be used by those within churches focused on signs and wonders. I first heard of this term in Mark Driscoll's book, *Doctrine*, (p. 386) and have chosen to include the term here to distinguish these churches and movements from those traditionally considered charismatic or Pentecostal. In my opinion *Charismania* is nearly identical to what is known as the NAR. However, NAR theology is not just limited to signs and wonders or spiritual gifts. Nevertheless, NAR leaders almost unanimously teach that signs and wonders flow from their theological system and teaching.

14 Bill Johnson Q&A, "Is it Always God's Will to Heal Someone?", n.d. http://bjm.org/qa/is-it-always-gods-will-to-heal-someone/.

15 Martyn Wendell Jones, "Inside the Popular Controversial Bethel Church," *Christianity Today*, April 24, 2016, http://www.christianitytoday.com/ct/2016/may/cover-story-inside-popular-controversial-bethel-church.html.

16 Ibid.

17 Chronicle, "Diamonds 'Rain' in Church," June 18, 2014, http://www.chronicle.co.zw/diamonds-rain-in-church/.

18 A personal account shared with me by a different friend who attended Bethel Church and School of Supernatural Ministry in Redding, California, circa 2012.

more, they believe that Apostles and Prophets still exist today, and are necessary for the church.

The Charis Fellowship Position from the Commitment to Common Identity[19]—We affirm that the Holy Spirit's works of baptizing,[20] sealing,[21] and indwelling[22] occur simultaneously with regeneration and are the possession of every true believer. The Holy Spirit gives each believer a unique combination of spiritual gifts for serving God and people.[23]

As we consider the work of the Holy Spirit today, we desperately need an agreed-upon set of definitions regarding what theological camps believe what. From here we can begin to discuss the particulars of each camp and evaluate them with the Scriptures. Next, we will consider the definition of signs and wonders.

[Figure 1.1]

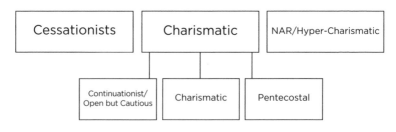

---

19 Given the lack of a specific definition within the Charis Fellowship it is difficult to state exactly where we land. My personal opinion is that a majority are in the cessationist camp, a significant and perhaps growing number in the continuationist camp, and a few are charismatic.

20 1 Cor. 12:13.

21 Eph. 1:13.

22 Rom. 8:11.

23 Rom. 12:6; 1 Cor. 12:7–11.

2
DEFINING
SIGNS AND WONDERS

To define signs and wonders, we need to first consider what these words mean when they occur separately. From there we can turn our attention toward synthesizing those individual definitions and define what they mean when they are used together.

Sign (σημεῖα): The word *sign*, apart from *wonders*, is used in the New Testament 62 times.[1] *Bauer's Greek-English Dictionary* (BDAG) defines this word as a "sign or distinguishing mark whereby something is known."[2] In the New Testament a sign or signs can be miraculous or non-miraculous events that have a special meaning, though this word is most frequently used to refer to miraculous events.

---

1 Matt. 12:38, 39(3), 16:1, 16:3, 16:4(3), 24:3, 24:30, 26:48; Mark 8:11, 8:12(2), 13:4, 16:7, [16:20]; Luke 2:12, 2:24, 11:16, 11:29(3), 11:30, 21:17, 21:11, 21:25, 23:8; John 2:11, 2:18, 2:23, 3:2, 4:48, 4:54, 6:2, 6:14, 6:26, 6:30, 7:31, 9:16, 10, 41:11:47, 12:18, 12:37, 20:30; Acts 2:19, 4:16, 4:22, 8:6, 8:13; Rom. 4:11; 1 Cor. 1:22, 14:22; 2 Cor. 2:12, 2 Thess. 3:17; Rev. 12:1, 12:3, 13:13, 13:14, 15:1, 16:14, 19:20.

2 William Arndt et al., *A Greek-English Lexicon of the New Testament and Other Early Christian Literature* (BDAG) (Chicago: University of Chicago Press, 2000), 920. The Louw Nida dictionary (Johannes P. Louw and Eugene Albert Nida, *Greek-English Lexicon of the New Testament: Based on Semantic Domains* (New York: United Bible Societies, 1996), 33.477) adds that a "sign" is "an event which is regarded as having some special meaning "and the Theological Dictionary of the New Testament (Gerhard Kittel, Gerhard Friedrich, and Geoffrey William Bromiley, *Theological Dictionary of the New Testament* (Grand Rapids, MI: W.B. Eerdmans, 1985), 1018–1019.)) states, a "sign demonstrates the truth of the message...serves a purpose of confirmation...[and] does not have to be a miraculous or apocalyptic sign..."

For example, Matthew's first use of the word *sign* occurs in verse 12:38. He writes, "then some of the scribes and Pharisees answered him, saying, 'Teacher, we wish to see a sign from you.'" In this instance, the Pharisees are requesting that Jesus perform some miraculous act to prove himself to be true. In 1 Corinthians 1:22, the Apostle Paul uses the word *sign* in an identical way when he writes, "Jews demand signs and Greeks wisdom." The Apostle John uses the word *sign(s)* more than any other New Testament writer, and exclusively uses it in reference to miraculous acts. The word occurs 17 times in his gospel account and seven times in the book of Revelation.

Writing about the entire purpose of his gospel account, in John 20:30–31, John says that Jesus did many signs "in the presence of the disciples" and indicates the reason he recorded the ones he did was "so that you may believe that Jesus is the Christ" (v. 20:31). The signs that John records are miraculous signs intended to have a special meaning or give specific confirmation that Jesus Christ is the Messiah.

The word *sign* is also used to speak of non-miraculous events that have a special meaning. Luke writes in 2:12, "And this will be a sign for you: you will find a baby wrapped in swaddling cloths and lying in a manger." Here the word *sign* points to a non-miraculous event that has special meaning. Despite all the miraculous things taking place during the birth of Christ, there was nothing supernatural about Mary wrapping Jesus in swaddling cloths and laying him in a manger. However, this detail would be a confirmation for the shepherds that they had found the right baby!

Matthew uses the word *sign* to speak of a non-miraculous event that had special meaning as well in 26:48. There he writes, "Now the betrayer had given them a sign, saying, 'the one I will kiss is the man, seize him.'" Again, there was nothing miraculous about Judas kissing Jesus; however, the kiss had a special meaning and confirmed to the soldiers whom they should arrest.

In Romans 4:11, the Apostle Paul uses the word *sign* for a non-miraculous event or action that has special meaning. On this occasion, he was speaking of circumcision as a "seal of righteousness." There was nothing physically miraculous in Abraham's circumcision; however, the act had special meaning in that it signified his faith in the promises of God.

Similarly, Paul also uses the word *sign* in 2 Thessalonians 3:17, writing, "This is the sign of the genuineness in every letter of mine; it is the way I write." Physiologically speaking, there was nothing miraculous about Paul writing this letter, but it did convey a special significance and meaning to his audience.

The word *sign* in the New Testament is most commonly used to describe miraculous events that have a special meaning. However, the word *sign* is also used, though much less frequently, to describe non-miraculous events or actions that have a special meaning.

Wonders (τέρατα): In the New Testament, with one possible exception in Acts 2, the word *wonders* never appears apart from *signs* and is defined as "something that astounds because of transcendent association."[3] Regarding this possible exception, contextual clues lead one to see that Peter added *and signs* to his quotation of Joel 2:28–32 to further define the scope of fulfillment that Joel predicted and that Peter is declaring has come.

For the specific purpose of gospel proclamation, the word *wonders* is used in combination with *signs* to confirm both the authenticity of the message being spoken and the messenger who is speaking. Significantly, with Acts 2:19 as the only possible exception, the word *wonders* never appears apart from the word *signs*. There is also no command anywhere in the New Testament that wonders are to be sought after or chased.

Signs and Wonders (σημεῖα καὶ τέρατα, τέρατα καὶ σημεῖα): We will see in chapter three that *signs and wonders* (or *wonders and signs*) occur together 15 times in the New Testament. When used together to refer to miraculous events that took place, these words confirm both the authenticity of the message and the messenger. In Acts,

---

3 BDAG, 999.

signs, and wonders, "mark the new age of eschatological redemption … typologically demonstrating that the predicted eschatological age has come."[4]

However, these words do not exclusively refer to an authorized messenger who delivered authorized messages. Negatively, *signs and wonders* will be used by the Antichrist to lead people away from faith in Jesus Christ. The TDNT (*Theological Dictionary of the New Testament*) states, that in the Gospels *signs and wonders* "are part of the pseudo-messiahs [that will come], although this does not rule out their performance by the true Messiah."[5]

Positively, *signs and wonders* were miraculous acts performed by believers to confirm that they spoke authoritatively for God and that their message was true. These miraculous acts were performed by Jesus, the Apostles, Moses (in the Old Testament), and three non-Apostles: Stephen, Phillip, and Barnabas.

In chapter three, we look at each instance where *signs and wonders* are used together in the New Testament. From there we will make observations about what the biblical authors write and begin to draw some working conclusions.

---

4 Ibid., 1020.
5 Ibid., 1019–1020.

3

THE TEXT

As with any legitimate study of the Bible we must first ask ourselves, "What does the text say?" We are trying to learn from the text what God has revealed, rather than find verses to confirm what we want to be true.

Below are all the occurrences in the New Testament where signs and wonders appear. From here, we will make some observations and working conclusions based on what we have seen thus far and consider in more detail exactly who is credited with performing signs and wonders.

Textual Occurrences

Matthew 24:24
"For false christs and false prophets will arise and perform great *signs and wonders,* so as to lead astray, if possible, even the elect." [1]

Mark 13:22
"For false christs and false prophets will arise and perform *signs and wonders,* to lead astray, if possible, the elect."

John 4:48
"So Jesus said to him, 'Unless you see *signs and wonders* you will not believe.'"

---

1 Emphasis mine.

TO EACH IS GIVEN

Acts 2:22

"Men of Israel, hear these words: Jesus of Nazareth, a man attested to you by God with mighty works and *wonders and signs* that God did through him in your midst, as you yourselves know."

Acts 2:43

"And awe came upon every soul, and many *wonders and signs* were being done through the apostles."

Acts 4:30

"...while you stretch out your hand to heal, and *signs and wonders* are performed through the name of your holy servant Jesus."

Acts 5:12

"Now many *signs and wonders* were regularly done among the people by the hands of the apostles. And they were all together in Solomon's Portico."

Acts 6:8

"And Stephen, full of grace and power, was doing great *wonders and signs* among the people."

Acts 7:36

"This man [Moses] led them out, performing *wonders and signs* in Egypt and at the Red Sea and in the wilderness for forty years."

Acts 14:3

"So they remained for a long time, speaking boldly for the Lord, who bore witness to the word of his grace, granting *signs and wonders* to be done by their hands."

Acts 15:12

"And all the assembly fell silent, and they listened to Barnabas and Paul as they related what *signs and wonders* God had done through them among the Gentiles."

Romans 15:19

"...by the power of *signs and wonders,* by the power of the Spirit of God—so that from Jerusalem and all the way around to Illyricum I have fulfilled the ministry of the gospel of Christ..."

2 Corinthians 12:12

"The signs of a true apostle were performed among you with utmost patience, with *signs and wonders* and mighty works."

2 Thessalonians 2:9

"The coming of the lawless one is by the activity of Satan with all power and false *signs and wonders*…"

Hebrews 2:4

"while God also bore witness by *signs and wonders* and various miracles and by gifts of the Holy Spirit distributed according to his will."

Textual Observations

In the Gospels

• Matthew and Mark both record Jesus' words that signs and wonders will be performed by false christs and false prophets (Matt. 24:24; Mark 13:22).

In Acts

• Luke does not use *signs and wonders* to describe what took place in Acts 2:1-41 when the Holy Spirit filled those waiting together in the upper room.

• Stephen, Phillip, and Barnabas are the only three non-Apostles recorded to perform *signs and wonders*. Stephen performs them before a Jewish audience, Phillip before a Samaritan audience, and Barnabas, with Paul, before a Gentile audience.

• After the Jerusalem Council in Acts 15, Luke never again uses *signs and wonders* together, nor the words individually in Acts, and Scripture is silent regarding *signs and wonders* with four exceptions found in the Epistles.

In the Epistles

• In Romans 15:19 and 2 Corinthians 12:12, Paul defends his apostleship by appealing to the *signs and wonders* that he performed.

• In 2 Thessalonians 2:9, Paul indicates that the Antichrist will come in power and with *signs and wonders*.

To Each Is Given

- *Signs and wonders* are never commanded to be performed, rather, they were reported to have been performed, and only by the Apostle Paul.
- Paul never commands Timothy to perform *signs and wonders* or to teach others to perform *signs and wonders*. Instead, Paul instructs Timothy to "not neglect the gift[2] you have, which was given you by prophecy when the council of elders laid their hands on you" (1 Tim. 4:14). While there is no specific gift listed by Paul, it is significant that Paul uses the word *gift*[3] rather than instructing Timothy to not neglect the s*igns and wonders* he was given by the laying on of the elders' hands.
- Paul never uses the phrase *signs and wonders* in 1 Corinthians 12, Romans 12, or Ephesians 4 while writing about spiritual gifts.
- Peter, who is credited with performing *signs and wonders* in the book of Acts, never uses the words *signs and wonders* when writing about spiritual gifts in 1 Peter 4:10–11.
- Hebrews 2:4 states that God bore witness to the gospel message by *signs and wonders* and *signs and wonders* appear to be listed as a separate category, distinct from spiritual gifts in Hebrews 2:4.

Who is Said to Perform Signs and Wonders?
- Moses (Acts 7:36)
- False christs and prophets (Matt. 24:24; Mark 13:22; 2 Thess. 2:9)
- Jesus (Acts 2:22)
- The Apostles (Acts 2:43; 5:12; 2 Cor. 12:12)
- Stephen (Acts 6:8)
- Phillip (implied from Acts 8:12–13)
- Barnabas (Acts 14:3; 15:12)
- Paul (Rom. 15:19, 2 Cor. 12:12)
- God (Heb. 2:4)

---

2 Gk. Χαρίσματος.

3 The same word Paul uses in 1 Cor. 12:4.

Conclusions

- *Signs and wonders* are a confirming mark of apostolic authority and the gospel message these men proclaimed.
- *Signs and wonders* are never prescriptively commanded of believers and should not be sought after by those in the church.
- *Signs and wonders* are not the gifts of the Holy Spirit.

Thus far, we have considered the definitions of the major positions regarding *signs and wonders* and spiritual gifts. We have considered how the words *sign*, *wonders,* and *signs and wonders* appear and are used in the New Testament. We have also looked at every instance that the words *signs* and *wonders* are used in the New Testament and have observed and drawn some working conclusions about how best to synthesize the biblical data. Next, we will consider in greater detail who performed signs and wonders, giving particular attention to the three non-Apostles who are recorded as doing so.

4
WHO PERFORMED SIGNS AND WONDERS

Two things became clear in the process of understanding the definition and purpose of signs and wonders: (1) relatively speaking, signs and wonders were not written about all that often, and (2) most often in the New Testament, it is either Jesus or the Apostles who are credited with performing signs and wonders, with three specific exceptions.

Tom, my pastor in college, who later became my boss, and I were out to lunch one day at The Great Wall enjoying some of the best Chinese food Warsaw, Indiana, had to offer. During our meal, we were discussing what I had been studying and learning regarding signs and wonders, and I shared with him that it appeared that signs and wonders were exclusively done by Jesus or the Apostles with three limited exceptions. Not one to miss an opportunity to insist on logic, Pastor Tom quickly pointed out that you can't have something be exclusive while acknowledging exceptions exist!

I didn't have a good answer to his challenge. It seemed logical to me that if *I* wanted signs and wonders to be limited to the work of the Apostles (isn't this what Acts 5:12 says?), and therefore not for the church today, then declaring that to be true was the best thing to do! However, standing in the way of that declaration was the reality that it wasn't exclusively true. It wasn't just Jesus and the Apostles, it was three other men as well: Stephen, Phillip, and Barnabas.

As I continued to study and wrestle with his observation, my presuppositions, and God's Word, I discovered something I hadn't seen before. Yes, Stephen, Phillip, and Barnabas were not Apostles, and yes, they are credited with performing signs and wonders. However, God empowered them to perform signs and wonders for a specific reason, in front of specific audiences as He confirmed that they spoke authoritatively for Him and that their message was true.

Stephen

The signs and wonders that Stephen performed authenticated him as an authorized messenger before a Jewish audience. Luke tells us in Acts 6:8, "And Stephen, full of grace and power, was doing great wonders and signs among the people." Stephen would, just a few verses later, stand before the high priest and give a Christ-centered interpretation of Israel's history and lose his life for doing so.

Before being stoned to death, Stephen declared that the Jewish leaders were "stiff-necked people, uncircumcised in heart and ears" (7:51). They were guilty of killing not only those who announced beforehand the coming of the Righteous One but also the Righteous One Himself (7:52). Through signs and wonders, God authenticated Stephen as a messenger, who was speaking a true message—before his Jewish audience. Sadly, rather than listening to the good news that Stephen preached, these leaders took his life.

Phillip

Phillip, while never directly credited with performing signs and wonders, did *signs and great miracles*. Based on the context of Acts 8, it would be a stretch to interpret *signs and great miracles* as meaning something different from Luke's use of the words *signs and wonders* elsewhere.[1]

Like Stephen, Phillip's audience is of great significance. Luke tells us in Acts 8:4-5, "Now those who were scattered went about preaching the word. Phillip went down to the city of Samaria and proclaimed

---

1 While it may be said that this line of reasoning is "special pleading," we must note that to remove Philip as a performer of signs and wonders only strengthens the case that signs and wonders were limited to the Apostles and now *two* other men (the church's first martyr and Barnabas, while serving alongside the Apostle Paul). Regardless of the position taken concerning Phillip, it is indisputable to see that at most only three, non-Apostles are credited with performing signs and wonders.

to them the Christ." [2] The non-apostle Stephen performed *signs and wonders* in front of a Jewish audience, and the non-apostle Phillip performed *signs and great miracles* in front of a Samaritan audience. Here, God was giving witness to the Samaritans and authenticating His word through the *signs and wonders* performed by Phillip.

In Acts 8:6, Luke records that "the crowds with one accord paid attention to what was being said by Phillip when they heard him and saw the signs he did." Phillip performed signs and wonders, and their purpose was to authenticate that his message was from God.

Barnabas

The third non-apostle to perform *signs and wonders* is Barnabas (alongside the Apostle Paul). Luke writes in Acts 14:3, "So they remained for a long time, speaking boldly for the Lord, who bore witness to the word of his grace, granting signs and wonders to be done by their hands." In Acts 14:3, we see that God is giving witness to the bold speaking of His word through the *signs and wonders* that Barnabas and Paul performed. Once again, God is authenticating His message and His messengers through *signs and wonders*.

In Acts 15:12, we see a slight shift in that God is now authenticating the audience for whom the *signs and wonders* were performed. Here, Luke tells us, "And all the assembly fell silent, and they listened to Barnabas and Paul as they related what signs and wonders God had done through them among the Gentiles."

Acts 15 records a watershed moment in the life of the early church. Luke sets the stage for us in Acts 15:1–2, writing,

> But some men came down from Judea and were teaching the brothers, "Unless you are circumcised according to the custom of Moses, you cannot be saved." And after Paul and Barnabas had no small dissension and debate with them, Paul and Barnabas and some of the others were appointed to go to Jerusalem to the apostles and the elders about this question.

---

2 Note the emphasis on the preaching of the word. Luke does not tell us that they went about performing signs and wonders for the sake of performing signs and wonders. The proclamation of the Word was central to their actions.

To Each Is Given

The question before the Jerusalem Council was whether or not faith alone in Jesus Christ was sufficient for salvation, or if one must also have confidence in the flesh (Phil. 3:4) by adding works according to the custom of Moses (i.e., works of the law, Gal. 2:15–3:14). This was a serious question and one that had tremendous significance for the early church, as it does for the church today.

During the debate among the Apostles and elders in Jerusalem, Peter stood up and declared, "Brothers, you know that in the early days God made a choice among you, that by my mouth the Gentiles should hear the word of the gospel and believe. And God, who knows the heart, bore witness to them, by giving them the Holy Spirit just as He did to us, and he made no distinction between us and them, having cleansed their hearts by faith" (Acts 15:7–9). After Peter speaks, concluding that "we will be saved through the grace of the Lord Jesus, just as they will," (v. 11) Barnabas and Paul related the *signs and wonders* God had done among the Gentiles (v. 12).

In Acts 14:3, *signs and wonders* authenticated to a Gentile audience that the messengers (Paul and Barnabas) and the message (the word of grace) they were preaching was from God. In Acts 15:12, Barnabas and Paul relate to the Jewish leaders how God confirmed both their message and them as messengers before a Gentile audience.

After this testimony from Barnabas and Paul, James makes a few more important points and the Jerusalem Council officially decides to not "trouble those of the Gentiles who turn to God" (v. 19). The Jerusalem Council concluded that Gentile believers are every bit as saved as Jewish believers. With the Apostles and elders in Jerusalem God also used the presence of *signs and wonders* as confirmation that His plan of salvation is for all kinds of people. Regardless of ethnicity, salvation is by grace alone, through faith alone, in the Lord Jesus alone.

Significantly, after the Jerusalem Council in Acts 15, Luke does not use the term *signs and wonders* again in the book of Acts. Throughout the rest of Paul's travels, as recorded by Luke or written about by Paul, *signs and wonders* are only mentioned twice as evidence confirming the ministry of the Apostle Paul (Rom. 15:19, 2 Cor. 12:12). In the New Testament, the only three non-apostles to perform signs and wonders were Stephen, Phillip, and Barnabas. Stephen did so before a Jewish audience, Philip before a Samaritan audience, and Barnabas before a Gentile audience.

It is my belief that these three men performed signs and wonders because God uniquely used them to begin the fulfillment of the disciples' mission from Acts 1:8.[3] Furthermore, after the Jerusalem Council, God limited the occurrences of signs and wonders to the Apostles (though Paul alone is credited with *signs and wonders* after this point) because now the gospel had taken root in Jerusalem, Samaria, and was confirmed with the Gentiles: the "ends of the earth."

The list of individuals who are credited with performing signs and wonders is incredibly small. It includes God, Moses, Jesus, the Apostles, Stephen, Philip, and Barnabas. The purpose of these *signs and wonders* was to authenticate both these men as God's messengers and their message. As we move forward from the definition and purpose of *signs and wonders*, we will now look at the other places in the New Testament where *signs and wonders* are recorded. Next, we turn our attention to Hebrews 2:4, where the author of this epistle uses both the phrases *signs and wonders* and *gifts of the Holy Spirit* to describe God's work of giving witness to the message of the Gospel.

---

3 Acts 1:8, "But you will receive power when the Holy Spirit has come upon you, and you will be my witnesses in Jerusalem and in all Judea and Samaria, and to the end of the earth."

5
HEBREWS 2:4

Hebrews 2:4 is an important passage with the potential to offer a clear distinction between signs and wonders and spiritual gifts. In fact, if the following interpretation of Hebrews 2:4 is in error, then much of what I argue in this book may be less certain.[1]

The question we must ask is, does the author of Hebrews make a distinction in verse 2:4 between signs and wonders, various miracles, and gifts of the Holy Spirit when he writes, "...while God also bore witness by signs and wonders and various miracles and by gifts of the Holy Spirit distributed according to his will"?

As we look at Hebrews 2:4, we must begin with the words written by the author of Hebrews and allow the Scriptures to convey the author's original intent. To do this, we must also understand this passage within the context of what has already been written.

The author of Hebrews, since 1:1, has been making the point that Jesus is greater than everything in every way. In verses 1–3 alone, the author articulates 10 different truths about the supremacy and greatness of Christ. The author writes that Christ is:

- The one God has spoken through in these last days—1:2
- The Son—1:2
- The heir of all things—1:2
- The Creator of the world—1:2
- The radiance of the glory of God—1:3

---

1 The conclusions I present are not entirely dependent on this understanding of Heb. 2:4, but they are greatly informed by the interpretation of the passage.

- The exact imprint of God's nature—1:3
- The one upholding the universe by the word of His power—1:3
- The one who made purification for sins—1:3
- The one now sitting at the right hand of the Majesty on high—1:3
- The one who is superior to the angels—1:4

In verses 5–14 the author begins to support the argument made in 1:4 by citing seven Old Testament passages. The message is clear: Jesus is greater than the angels. To be sure, angels have their place as "ministering spirits sent out to serve" (v. 1:14), but they are not the "Son." As a result of the greatness of the Son, "we must pay closer attention to what we have heard, lest we drift away from it" (Heb. 2:1). While God had previously spoken through the prophets, now He has spoken through His Son. God has spoken, we must listen!

Continuing in Hebrews 2:2, we read that "the message declared by angels has been proven to be reliable, and every transgression or disobedience received a just retribution." Here, the author of Hebrews introduces both an example and a warning that he will frequently return to, especially in chapters 3 and 4.

The Israelites who left Egypt with Moses serve as an example for his readers in that they were unable to enter rest (i.e. the promised land) because of their unbelief (Heb. 3:19). The warning is that those who hear the gospel message today still face the same disastrous consequences as unbelieving Israel if they fail to listen. We will not escape if we "neglect such a great salvation" (Heb. 2:3).

Pressing his argument one step further, the author of Hebrews then states that this salvation message was "declared first by the Lord, and it was attested to us by those who heard" (Heb. 2:3). However, it was not only "those who heard" who bore witness to the message of salvation, it was also God Himself, and He did so through "signs and wonders, various miracles, and gifts of the Holy Spirit." What becomes clear from the context surrounding Hebrews 2:4 is that God has, alongside Christ and the Apostles, provided witness to the salvation message in a variety of ways.

In thinking back to the Gospel accounts of Jesus's life and ministry, along with the early church in the book of Acts, we can see God's authenticating witness being demonstrated through the many miracles that Jesus performed and through the signs and wonders credited to the Apostles. In Acts, Luke records numerous times, until Acts 16, that the Apostles did signs and wonders.[2] Through these men, the good news of the gospel that Jesus and the Apostles preached, was attested to by God through signs and wonders and various miracles.

Grammatically supporting the distinction between signs and wonders, various miracles, and gifts of the Holy Spirit is the presence and repetition of the word *and* (καὶ). This word functions as a coordinating conjunction and shows the relationship between two or more things that are separate and yet related. Here the word is used two specific times to show God as authenticating the gospel message in three distinct ways.

To illustrate this point, think of how we use the word *and* to describe meals we eat. We might say, "Last night at dinner, I ate steak and potatoes and broccoli." While all three foods were a part of the meal I ate, they are all distinct foods. Steak is not broccoli, nor are potatoes and broccoli the same even though they are both vegetables.

Similarly, the writer of Hebrews uses the word *and* to point to three distinct witnesses that God has used for his purposes. God gave witness with (1) signs and wonders, (2) various miracles, and (3) gifts of the Holy Spirit.[3]

At this point in the discussion we must ask whether *gifts of the Holy Spirit* are the same gifts Paul writes about in 1 Corinthians 12

---

2 Acts 2:43, 4:30, 5:12, 6:8, 7:36, [8:4-5], 14:3, 15:12.

3 Philippians 4:9 and Matthew 4:23 are also passages in which *and* functions the same way. In Philippians, the Apostle Paul writes, "What you have learned and received and heard and seen in me—practice these things ..." Here the repetition of the word *and* functions to show distinction within the group of words Paul uses. Learned, received, and heard are similar but not identical and the Apostle Paul uses them to describe differing parts of a whole. In Matthew 4:23, we have the word *and* separating each participle used to describe the action and activity of Jesus' ministry. Teaching, proclaiming, and healing are not the same things. However, they are collectively a part of the whole of Jesus' ministry.

and Romans 12. The phrase *gifts of the Holy Spirit* in Hebrews 2:4 is quite similar, but not identical, to what the Apostle Paul writes in 1 Corinthians 12:11. To compare the two passages, we must first make some general observations regarding 1 Corinthians 12.[4]

In 1 Corinthians 12, Paul begins addressing improper behavior within the church that arises from an incorrect understanding of the origin, empowerment, and purpose of spiritual gifts. When we arrive at verse 11, Paul uses the word *these* (ταῦτα) to cite all the gifts that he has just listed.

In verse 11, Paul summarizes his point from verses 3–10 that all gifts have been given by the Holy Spirit, and all gifts are empowered by the Holy Spirit. While these gifts vary in function, place of use, and result, all these gifts are "empowered by one and the same Holy Spirit, who apportions to each one individually as he wills."

Though all spiritual gifts are trinitarian in essence, we learn in verse 11 that God the Holy Spirit is the agent by whom gifts are given and through whom believers are empowered to use the gifts they have been given. Because the Holy Spirit is the direct agent of spiritual gifts, there is not a hierarchy of gifts within the church. There are no gifts that are more empowered than others, nor are there gifts that are better because they are of the Holy Spirit while others are not.

Comparing the last phrase of Hebrews 2:4, Romans 12:6, and 1 Corinthians 12:11 shows further similarities and a few important differences that must be noted.

Hebrews 2:4
"…while God also bore witness by signs and wonders and various miracles and by gifts of the Holy Spirit distributed according to his will."

Romans 12:6
"Having gifts that differ according to the grace given to us, let us use them…"

---

4 A more detailed exposition of this passage follows below.

1 Corinthians 12:11
"All these are empowered by one and the same Spirit, who apportions to each one individually as he wills."

First, we must note that the word *gifts* (χαρισμάτων) does not appear in the original language in Hebrews 2:4 or 1 Corinthians 12:11. Our English translations supply the word *gifts* based on the context of the passage. [5]

In Hebrews 2:4, the word *gifts* is supplied because of the word μερισμοῖς which means to "distribute or apportion."[6] In 1 Corinthians 12:11, the word *these* is used based on the broader context of what Paul has written in 1 Corinthians 12:1–10. Specifically, Paul uses the word *gifts* (χαρισμάτων) in verse 12:4 and verse 31.

Contextually then, *these* (ταῦτα) in verse 12:11 is referring to gifts. Thus, while Hebrews 2:4 and 1 Corinthians 12:11 do not specifically use the word *gifts,* the context of these passages indicates that *gifts* are in view.

Secondly, we must note that the word *Spirit* (πνεῦμα) does not occur in all three passages. Absent in Romans 12:3–8, where Paul addresses *gifts that differ,* is any direct reference to the Spirit. However, both God and Christ are directly referenced, and the context regarding believers being *members one of another* bears a striking resemblance to 1 Corinthians 12:12–27. As a result, it is reasonable to conclude that both lists identify spiritual gifts even if the Spirit is not directly referenced in Romans 12:3–8.

Thirdly, we must note that the word translated *will* in our English Bibles does not appear in Romans 12 and is a different Greek word in Hebrews 2:4 (θέλησιν) than it is in 1 Corinthians 12:11 (βούλεται). However, the idea of *will* is present in Romans 12:3 when Paul writes

---

5 The five main English translations (ESV, NIV, NASB95, CSB, KJV) all supply the word *gifts* as the object that has been distributed.

6 BDAG, 633 (i.e. of the various gifts proceeding from the Holy Spirit Hb 2:4.). See also Johannes P. Louw and Eugene Albert Nida, *Greek-English Lexicon of the New Testament Based on Semantic Domains.* (LN) (New York: United Bible Societies, 1996), 57.89.

of *God's assignment* and the word translated *assigned* (ἐμέρισεν) shares the same root word as *distributed* (μερισμοῖς) from Hebrews 2:4.

Regarding the will of God, βούλομαι means to plan a course of action,[7] while θέλησις means the act of willing.[8] In the New Testament these words are used to communicate the determined, purposed plan of God and what he wants or desires. Even though these two words are used to refer to different aspects of God's will, it would be incorrect to conclude that these two passages do not both speak to God's sovereign design and desire concerning spiritual gifts.

While we may desire that every passage had the words *gifts* or *Spirit* in it, it would be difficult to conclude that these three passages are not referring to spiritual gifts. However, despite some of the grammatical and linguistic differences between these passages, the congruity is apparent, and Hebrews 2:4 does appear to communicate a distinction between signs and wonders and spiritual gifts.

To my knowledge, the distinction between signs and wonders, various miracles, and gifts distributed by the Holy Spirit is not a distinction widely written about in conservative evangelical circles. As such, this reality should give us pause before reaching a conclusion that may not be widely shared among like-minded scholars and pastors.

Furthermore, I know of no one else who has specifically written or spoken about signs and wonders ceasing and spiritual gifts continuing. However, while not widely discussed, this distinction is communicated by the following men as they have written commentaries or preached on the Epistle to the Hebrews.

Theologian Homer Kent believes it is likely that signs and wonders, various miracles, and gifts of the Holy Spirit are different pieces of evidence of the gospel message. Kent writes,

> There was also divine confirmation of the message of salvation. By signs (supernatural occurrences which acted as

---

7 BDAG, 182. LN, 30.56.

8 BDAG, 447. TDNT, 319. LN, 25.1.

proofs or indicators) and wonders (supernatural acts which produced awe among beholders) and various miracles (a variety of displays of divine power), God indicated His involvement in the message of salvation. Many of these are recorded in Acts (e.g., 3:6–8; 5:12; 18–20; 6:8; 8:6; 9:33–34, 40–41, et al.)

Distributions of the Holy Spirit may be understood as God's bestowal of the Spirit upon each believer (treating "Holy Spirit" as an objective genitive). A supporting passage would be Galatians 3:5, "He that ministereth to you in Spirit, and worketh miracles among you...." With this understanding, according to his will would clearly refer to the Father, and perhaps should be construed not only with 'distributions of the Holy Spirit,' but also with 'signs and wonders and various miracles.' On the whole it seems *more likely* that Holy Spirit is a subjective genitive, and that the reference is to those Spirit produced evidences in men's lives which offer living proof of salvation. This truth is stated in 1 Corinthians 12:11, 'But all these worketh that one and the selfsame Spirit, dividing to every man severally as he will.' According to his will would then probably refer to the Spirit, although it could conceivably refer to the Father, with whose will all Persons of the godhead are always in perfect harmony. Pink notes that the act of distributing spiritual gifts is attributed in Scripture to the Father (1 Cor. 7:17), the Son (Eph. 4:7), and the Spirit (1 Cor. 12:11). Such a salvation, provided with strong authentication like this, leaves man without excuse for his neglect.[9]

Al Mohler, president of the Southern Baptist Theological Seminary, writes,

---

9 Homer Kent, *The Epistle to the Hebrews* (Winona Lake: BMH Books 2002), 50. Emphasis mine. Homer Kent formerly served as president of Grace Schools and is the brother of Wendell Kent who served as senior pastor at Waynesboro Grace Brethren for 12 years, the church I currently serve in.

Finally, the "gifts from the Holy Spirit" attest to the truthfulness of the gospel and its superiority over the message delivered by angels. Again, the author of Hebrews helps us strip away our misconceptions about why spiritual gifts exist. Spiritual gifts are not an end to themselves to be used for our personal, private enjoyment. Spiritual gifts edify the church (1 Cor 14: 3–5; Eph 4:11–12) and testify that Jesus Christ is Lord. As Paul explains in Ephesians 4:8, Christ has ascended on high, and now, with all authority in heaven, showers gifts on his church. Gifts within the church, therefore, bear witness to Jesus Christ as the resurrected Lord and to the superiority of the new covenant over the old.[10]

John Piper, in a sermon preached on Hebrews 2:1–4 in 1996, states,

The fourth witness in this series is again God himself. The sequence begins with God and ends with God. Verse 4: "God also bearing witness with them [that is, with the eyewitnesses], both by signs and wonders and by various miracles and by gifts of the Holy Spirit according to His own will." God spoke the great salvation into being through Jesus, and now God comes in again to witness to his own word and work.

The way he witnesses is through signs and wonders and miracles and gifts of the Holy Spirit. In other words, when the apostles came to preach and witness to what they had seen and heard, God enabled them to do miracles and he poured out on the new believers gifts of the Spirit. This was God's added testimony to the message of his great salvation.[11]

Textual notes from the ESV Study Bible indicate,

God also bore witness. God's witness came through miracles performed alongside the gospel's proclamation, confirm-

---

10 Al Mohler, *Christ-Centered Exposition Commentary: Exalting Jesus in Hebrews.* (Nashville: B&H Publishing, 2017) Loc. 775 of 5870, Kindle.

11 John Piper, "Spoken, Confirmed, Witnessed: A Great Salvation," *Desiring God,* May 5, 1996, https://www.desiringgod.org/messages/spoken-confirmed-witnessed-a-great-salvation.

ing it. The three terms *signs*, *wonders*, and *miracles* over-lap in meaning and thus should not be finely distinguished (they appear together in Acts 2:22; 2 Cor. 12:12; cf. 2 Thess. 2:9; and elsewhere "signs and wonders" are often connect-ed). *gifts*. "Apportionings," "distributions" (Gk. *merismos*) from the Holy Spirit. *distributed according to his will* (sic). This probably refers not just to the distribution of spiritual gifts (see, however, 1 Cor. 12:4–11, esp. verse 11) but also to all the works of God in Heb. 2:4; these are works done ac-cording to God's will, not of human volition (cf. Gal. 3:5).[12]

Again, while an exhaustive list of commentaries cannot be cited to support the conclusion that three distinct groups of witnesses are referenced in Hebrews 2:4, credible scholars and pastors do share this conclusion. By seeing these groups as closely related, and yet distinct, the conclusion that signs and wonders are not the same as spiritual gifts gains further biblical support.

Another helpful analogy may be that signs and wonders, various miracles, and spiritual gifts are like biological siblings. My three bi-ological children are closely related, and they share similarities with one another, yet they are distinct people. Their similarities are the re-sult of being from one common source. Their distinctions come from the unique ways their own DNA code was created and how that code has reproduced itself through their bodies. Similarly, signs and won-ders, various miracles, and spiritual gifts are similar because God is the source of each. However, they are also distinct. God has a unique plan and use for each of these categories and is confirming His word through their witness.

The theological implications that arise out of an understanding that signs and wonders are distinct from spiritual gifts are significant. Be-fore we move on to specifically consider spiritual gifts, it may be helpful to summarize the theological, and practical, implications that have been observed thus far:

---

12 David Chapman, ESV *Study Bible* (Crossway Publishing, 2008), n 2:4, 2363.

- Signs and wonders are restricted to the Apostles and their close associates (on a very limited basis).[13]

- Signs and wonders are not for the church today. They were limited to the Apostles and were used by God uniquely to confirm their apostolic authority. To this point we must note that neither the church nor its leaders are ever commanded to perform signs and wonders.

Regarding such signs and wonders in the church today, I contend that these present-day phenomena are false signs and wonders carried out by Satan (2 Thess. 2:9). In fact, this is one of the points the Apostle Paul makes in 2 Corinthians 11 regarding false apostles who are deceitful workmen. He indicates that they are disguising themselves as Apostles of Christ, "and no wonder, for even Satan disguises himself as an angel of light" (2 Cor. 11:13–15). Furthermore, I believe Satan would provide people with miraculous signs and wonders if this meant they would continue to follow leaders who would ultimately lead them away from Christ and true spiritual life and healing.[14]

By understanding that the New Testament makes a distinction between signs and wonders and spiritual gifts, we can correctly reject the errant claims and teaching that signs and wonders should be chased. However, we are also kept from throwing the baby out with the bathwater and simply rejecting spiritual gifts that appear to be similar to some of the recorded signs and wonders.

---

13 Incidentally, this point is principally the same as conclusions held regarding the New Testament authorship of Scripture, i.e., Mark was not an Apostle, but he was a close associate of the Apostle Peter, who commissioned Mark to write an account of the Gospel of Jesus Christ.

14 Regarding this bold claim, I fully recognize this conclusion is based on a new set of definitions that are introduced in this book. Therefore, there most certainly are churches and people who use the phrase *signs and wonders* and do so in a way that differs from the definition I have given. I am not saying that all churches who use the term *signs and wonders* are empowered by the activity of Satan. What I am saying is the groups who are specifically chasing signs and wonders today (as seen and documented within the NAR movement) are seeing supernatural phenomena done by the power of Satan. These NAR churches, who commendably want to experience God in powerful and personal ways, need to reevaluate their doctrine and practices.

Without question, some spiritual gifts look similar to some of the signs and wonders that occurred at the hands of the Apostles. However, because of the distinction that Hebrews 2:4 makes and the way the rest of the New Testament records the activity of signs and wonders, we can and should see a distinction between the two. As a result, we can conclude that God still gifts believers today with the spiritual gifts that are enumerated in the New Testament and that these gifts are different from what God did through the Apostles by signs and wonders.

6

SPIRITUAL GIFTS:
THEIR SOURCE AND PURPOSE

So far, we've noted the distinction between signs and wonders and spiritual gifts. In the New Testament, we see signs and wonders primarily performed at the hands of the Apostles, while spiritual gifts have been given to all believers within the church. We now direct our attention to this last point, considering in greater detail what Paul wrote in 1 Corinthians 12, Romans 12, and Ephesians 4, and how those passages apply to the church today.

As we look at 1 Corinthians 12 and what the Apostle Paul wrote to this church, we must first observe a few important details that will aid our interpretation. By doing so, we will be able to more accurately understand what Paul intended when he originally wrote this letter.

We first note that Paul is writing to a multi-ethnic church in the city of Corinth. In Acts 18:1–17, Luke records facts about Paul's initial visit to the city of Corinth and the church that was planted as a result. Notably, in verse 6 Luke tell us that Paul, after being opposed and reviled by the Jews, "shook out his garments and said to them, 'your blood be on your own heads! I am innocent. From now on I will go to the Gentiles.'" After this Paul went to Titus Justus's house which was next door to the synagogue and despite opposition from certain Jews, we are also told "Crispus, the ruler of the synagogue, believed in the Lord" and that "many of the Corinthians hearing Paul believed and were baptized" (18:6–8). In verse 11, Luke tells us that Paul stayed with this church for 18 months "teaching the word of God among them."

The second detail is that the English words *now concerning* (περί δὲ) appear several times in 1 Corinthians.[1] Given Paul's repeated use of this phrase it appears that he was addressing specific questions the Corinthian church had written to him. This would indicate that the Corinthians had questions about *spiritual gifts* (1 Cor. 12:1) and were writing to Paul asking for him to weigh in on the issue.

Thirdly, it is unnatural to the context of 1 Corinthians 12 to split up the list of gifts that Paul articulates, interpreting some gifts as enduring or permanent gifts, and other gifts as temporary *sign* gifts that no longer function in the church today.[2] Paul gives no indication in what he writes that he intends the Corinthian church to arrive at such a conclusion. Simply put, they would not have read his words and concluded that gifts *wisdom, knowledge, faith, prophecy,* and *distinguishing between spirits* were permanent while *gifts of healings, working of miracles, various tongues,* and the *interpretation of tongues* were temporary sign gifts.[3]

Now, to be fair to those who divide Paul's list of spiritual gifts into these two categories, we must recognize that they are often arguing against the abuses of spiritual gifts that are seen in many churches today. The claim by many hyper-charismatics, for example, that *gifts of healings* are guaranteed is one that should be rejected because it does not fit what Paul says about gifts in general or gifts of healings specifically. Gifts of healings are apportioned and empowered by the Holy Spirit as he wills, not as we will (1 Cor. 12:11).

---

1 7:1, 7:25, 8:1, 12:1, 16:1, 16:12.

2 John MacArthur, *1 Corinthians* (Chicago: Moody Bible Institute 1984), 297. Dr. John MacArthur is perhaps the most vocal proponent of this conclusion. I am incredibly grateful for the tremendous impact Dr. MacArthur's ministry has had on my life, but I believe his categories of "edifying gifts" and "sign gifts" are forced into the text. He writes, "A thorough examination will yield the truth that spiritual gifts fill two major purposes: the permanent gifts edify the church and the temporary gifts are signs to confirm the Word of God."

3 In first-hand conversations with those who have attended BSSM, I have learned that at least some within NAR circles see "words of wisdom" and "words of knowledge" as *sign* gifts, not edifying gifts. They believe that God spontaneously brings specific facts about a person's life to them so that they can shock a person into listening to the Gospel. I share this point here to simply illustrate how the term *sign gifts* can be defined differently between different theological camps.

Thus, while the conclusions and warnings by cessationists should be accepted, namely that spiritual gifts are not divinely enabled abilities to be god-like and heal at will, the path forward is not found by identifying some gifts as *sign gifts* and thereby declaring they no longer exist today.[4] Rather, the solution lies, in part, with seeing a distinction between signs and wonders and spiritual gifts.

Lastly, the argument that the Apostle Paul is making in 1 Corinthians 12 is that there is not a hierarchy of spiritual gifts or spiritual people within the church. D.A. Carson writes, "one conclusion is unavoidable: Paul tends to flatten distinctions between 'charismatic' gifts and 'noncharismatic' gifts in the modern sense of those terms."[5] Seeking to put an end to the Corinthian church's internal power struggles over which gifts (people) were greater, Paul flattens the list of gifts and drives his point home by writing the following:

1. "...it is the same God who empowers them all [gifts] in everyone" (1 Cor. 12:6).

2. "All these [gifts] are empowered by one and the same Spirit, who apportions to each one individually as he wills" (1 Cor. 12:11).

3. "For in one Spirit we were all baptized into one body..." (1 Cor. 12:13). This point is critical in understanding that there are not "really spiritual" people and "average spiritual" people in Corinth. Furthermore, the distinction between gifts is at the will of the Holy Spirit, not because some have received a greater portion of the Holy Spirit than others. All have been baptized into one body in the Holy Spirit. No distinction exists.

4. "God has arranged the members in the body, each one of them, as he chose" (1 Cor. 12:18). Here Paul is asserting that individuals should not look down on themselves if they have a gift that doesn't look as good as someone else's gift. "The foot cannot

---

4 Regarding 1 Cor. 14:22 and tongues being a sign, I will discuss this in greater detail in chapter 12.

5 D.A. Carson, *Showing the Spirit* (Grand Rapids: Baker Book House, 1989), 34.

say 'I do not belong' because I am not a hand" (1 Cor. 12:15). Because there is no hierarchy within the body of Christ a person must not conclude that they are less significant than another who may have a different gift or role.

5. "God has so composed the body ... that there may be no division in the body" (1 Cor. 12:25). The point Paul makes in verses 21–24 is that one cannot tell another that they are less important (or spiritual) if they have a gift that doesn't look as good, useful, or supernatural.

6. "God has appointed in the church ..." (1 Cor. 12:28). Once again, the Apostle Paul is making the point that how the body has been composed is at the appointment of God and his sovereign will.

Six times in 1 Corinthians 12, the Apostle Paul makes a statement about how the differences found within the body of Christ are the result of God's sovereign choice.[6] The conclusion is hard not to miss; if God has chosen to compose his body in this way, who are we to claim that some gifts (or people) are more special than others, or inversely, that some gifts (or people) are less special than others?

Verses 1–3

As we begin to look at the text specifically, we need to note that the word *gifts* in verse 1 is not a word that appears in the Greek text; it is supplied by our English translations.[7] The word that Paul wrote is πνευματικός. Occurring 15 times throughout 1 Corinthians, this word has a range of nuanced meaning.[8] However, even though the specific meaning of this word does seem to shift as Paul uses it through this letter, there is consistency in that all its uses that have to do with the Spirit. Ciampa and Rosner write, "BDAG and most translations support the key word as "spiritual gifts" or "those with spiritual gifts, but

---

6 Paul uses the words *empowers, empowered, were all baptized, arranged, composed*, and *appointed* to make his point clear.

7 The ESV does contain a footnote indicating that *spiritual persons* may also be an appropriate translation.

8 1 Cor. 2:13, 2:15, 3:1, 9:11, 10:3, 10:4, 12:1, 14:1, 14:37, 15:44, 15:46.

the word is much broader in its meaning ... in fact, in 12:1–3 Paul probably has in mind the difference between acting under the influence of other spiritual powers."[9]

In chapters 2 and 3, the context clearly demonstrates that the nuanced meaning of this word is *spiritual truths* and *people of the Spirit*.[10] In 9:11, the focus shifts to Paul's work among the Corinthian church and his right to reap *fleshly things* from them because he sowed *spiritual things* (πνευματικός) while among them.

In 10:3–4, the focus shifts yet again and is about the supernatural experiences the Israelites had as they ate manna and drank from the rock. Paul states that the food and drink they consumed was *spiritual* (πνευματικός) food and *spiritual* (πνευματικός) drink.

In 14:1 the word *gifts* (πνευματικός) is again supplied by our English translations, a decision that fits well within the context of what Paul is writing. However, in 14:37 the focus appears to shift away from *gifts* specifically and back toward a *spiritual* (πνευματικός) person. Lastly, in chapter 15, the word appears two final times and is used to define what type of resurrection, or *spiritual* (πνευματικός) *body*, believers will be given.

The point in highlighting all these occurrences is to demonstrate that throughout the book of 1 Corinthians the word πνευματικός is used to speak of the Spirit's involvement in a variety of ways. Thus, the choice in 12:1 to supply the word *gifts* as the object of *spiritual* is a contextual one. However, it is one that does not fit the context of verses 1–3.

Aiming for these brothers and sisters to be informed, Paul continues his explanation of spiritual gifts by first identifying the activities of *spiritual people*. When understood in the broader context beginning in chapter 8, what may seem like an odd way to begin his response is of tremendous significance.

In 8:1, using the same phrase as he did in 7:1 and 12:1, (περί δὲ) Paul begins to address questions that the church has regarding food

---

9 Roy Ciampa and Brian Rosner, *The First Letter to the Corinthians* (Grand Rapids: Eerdmans, 2011), 562.

10 BDAG, 837.

sacrificed to idols. Building his case throughout chapters 8, 9, and much of 10, Paul makes a stunning statement in 10:20. There he writes, "No, I imply that what pagans sacrifice they offer to demons and not to God." Pagan, or idol, worship is not indifferent to the things of God, nor is it simply uninformed and ignorant of who God is. Pagan worship is demonically inspired worship that is completely against the things of God.

Based on what we know of the city of Corinth, and what Paul writes about in chapter 10, it is plausible to understand that there were people in the Corinthian church who were performing miracles or even claiming supernatural revelation who did not acknowledge that Jesus is Lord.

This is why Paul writes in 1 Corinthians 12:3, "Therefore I want you to understand that no one speaking in the Spirit of God ever says 'Jesus is accursed!' and no one can say 'Jesus is Lord' except in the Holy Spirit." As Paul begins to explain what spiritual gifts are, he first wants them to understand who *people of the Spirit* are.[11]

Verses 4-6

Shifting from pagan idol worshipers, Paul next turns his attention to true believers and the different gifts that God the Holy Spirit gives to them. Beginning in verse 4, he writes, "Now there are varieties or gifts,[12] but the same Spirit; and there are varieties of service, but the same Lord; and there are varieties of activities, but it is the same God who empowers them all in everyone." Paul's main point in verses 4-6 may be expressed in two subpoints: (1) there is sovereignty over the variety of gifts, (2) there is unity amid the variety of gifts.

The word variety means division, distribution, or apportionment and is used by Paul three times to highlight the sovereignty of God's spiritual gifts.[13] Later in verse 11 Paul will use the verb form of this

---

11 See Appendix B for the checklist I use to evaluate various sources regarding their approach to spiritual gifts.

12 Gk. Χαρισμάτων.

13 BDAG, 229. The noun form of this word occurs only these three times in the NT.

word to reiterate God's sovereignty over the gifts, writing that the Spirit "apportions to each one individually as he wills." God is sovereign over spiritual gifts. Spiritual gifts will not look exactly the same within the body, and even two people who may have the same gift may find the Spirit empowering its use in a variety of ways.

However, despite the variety that exists because of the sovereign design of God, there is also unity amid the variety. In the text this unity is highlighted by the repetition of the word *same* three different times.

Furthermore, by using the name of each member of the Trinity, Paul highlights this unity by first directing our attention to each member of the Godhead. [14] They are not only the source of spiritual gifts; they are the united example for the body to follow.

The word *gifts* (χάρισμα) is transliterated in English as charisma. This is where we get our word charismatic from, and it is most simply defined as gifts of grace.[15] In verse 8, Paul will outline the variety of gifts that have been given, however, here he first highlights that a sovereign and unified distinction exists between all the gifts.

The word *service* (διακονία) is defined as service or ministry and is where we get our English word *deacon* from.[16] The point here is that there are a variety of places where the gifts will be used and that even the same gifts may be used in different areas of ministry or service. Yet, this too is because of the sovereign design of God, and it is the same Lord!

At my church we see this verse lived out nearly every week during our Sunday School hour. Like most churches we have classes available for children and adults and need many different people to teach these classes. As these people teach, they are using gifts they have been given by God to serve in different places. Often times, the im-

---

14 Carson, *Showing the Spirit,* 33. Carson adds a note of caution, "it would be wrong to think that the connections are exclusive: as if the Spirit gives only distributions of gifts, the Lord Jesus gives only distributions of service, and so forth."

15 BDAG, 1081 "of special gifts of a non-material sort, bestowed through God's generosity on individual Christians."

16 Ibid., 230 "functioning in the interest of a larger public, service, office."

pactful adult teachers would not do well in a children's class, and vice versa. However, these individuals should not conclude that one area of ministry is more significant or honoring to the Lord than another. Each has been given not only a gift but an area of ministry to use that gift in.

In verse 6, Paul uses the word *activities* (ἐνέργημα) to highlight a third aspect to the variety and unity that exists. This word focuses on the results of what takes place when a gift is used. [17] While the word *activities* is certainly a good one, we might also use the word *effects* or *workings* as well.[18] The point here is that God is in control of the results as we use our gifts and the same gift will be empowered by God in a variety of ways.

Think again of the gift of teaching and the distinction that exists among teachers who faithfully serve their local churches and teachers who are empowered by God to serve a wider audience. God is in control of the results as we use our gifts, just as he is in control of where we use our gifts and what gifts we have been given.

In contrast to demonically empowered pagan worship, true worshipers are empowered by the triune God and have gifts that differ from one another. Yet, despite the distinctions between the gifts received, the places they are used, and the effects of their use, it is the same God who empowers them all.

Verses 7–12

Given the struggles that the Corinthian church is said to have and their propensity toward division along party lines (namely some "follow Paul" while others "follow Apollos," 1 Cor. 3:4) what Paul says in verse 7 is paradigm-changing. Paul writes, "to each is given a manifestation of the Spirit for the common good." From what we learn in verses 1–6 of chapter 12, accompanied with what Paul writes in 3:4, we continue to see the picture of this church emerge.

The Corinthians were young, immature believers, who often thought of one another in a fleshly way (1 Cor. 3:1). They easily di-

---

17 Ibid., 335 "activity as expression of capability, activity,"
18 Cf. 12:10 "workings" (ἐνέργημα)

vided themselves and missed the truth that what unites them in Christ is greater than what distinguishes them regarding who proclaimed the gospel to them, or who baptized them (1 Cor. 1:10–17). They also lacked the spiritual discernment to understand that while there may be people who do *spiritual things*, if those people do not claim Jesus as Lord, they are to be rejected. Lastly, in verses 4–6 we see Paul flatten spiritual gifts by crediting their source within the triune God, not the greatness of any one person.

Through verse 7, Paul continues to hammer the point home that spiritual gifts are subject to the will of God and as a result we should not elevate some gifts or people above others. The word *each* (ἑκάστῳ) means one of an aggregate in a distributive sense.[19] It conveys the idea that everyone in the church receives something from God.

For example, if I said "I gave each of my four children one dollar for their allowance yesterday" I mean that all my kids, the totality in a distributive sense, received one dollar from me. Verse 7 begins with Paul clearly asserting that the entire Corinthian church, and by extension, all believers everywhere, are given something.

The word *given* (δίδοται) is a present, passive, indicative verb that tells us that each person in the church has received something. This type of verb is called a "divine passive" since "the subject is being acted upon … with God as the stated or implied agent."[20] What they have received is a manifestation of the Spirit. It is not the wealthy who give to the poor, or those a part of higher social classes that are benevolent to those beneath them. No, God himself is giving to all regardless of wealth, social status, age, or cultural prestige.

The word *manifestation* (φανέρωσις) means "disclosure or an announcement."[21] The gift they have received is *of the Spirit* and reveals that the Spirit is at work. The point Paul is making is that believers in the Corinthian church have equally received a manifestation of the

---

19 BDAG, 298.

20 Michael S. Heiser and Vincent M. Setterholm, *Glossary of Morpho-Syntactic Database Terminology* (Lexham Press, 2013), 2013.

21 BDAG, 1049.

Spirit from God "who empowers them all [the gifts] in everyone" (1 Cor. 12:6b).

F.F. Bruce notes, "there is no warrant for saying that one gift manifests his presence more than another."[22] We cannot claim that some spiritual gifts show more of the Spirit than other gifts do. The Spirit is equally revealed by everyone who has been given a gift by God.

The last part of verse 7 also provides a great service in that it plainly tells us that spiritual gifts are for the common good. The word translated *common good* is (συμφέρον) and means to be "advantageous."[23] The point here is that spiritual gifts are not for the self-promotion, benefit, or praise of an individual but for the advantage of the church.

The purpose of spiritual gifts is for the body of believers to be built up (1 Cor. 14:3) not simply for an individual to possess divine power or be the primary beneficiary.[24] Each believer has been given a spiritual gift that reveals the Spirit, and this is for the benefit of other believers. Individuals certainly may benefit from the use of their spiritual gifts, but they do so in the context of those gifts being used to serve others, not themselves.

As we seek to define these gifts, we must keep in mind that no specific definition is given in Scripture for each gift nor is one complete list of gifts ever given. These two realities should give us pause as we seek to define what each gift is, and we must be careful not to press our definitions beyond what Scripture will allow.

Also, we should not place undue significance on any one gift, believing it to be better than another. To make this error would be to fall into the same trap the Corinthian church had fallen in to. Before specifically considering and defining each spiritual gift, it may be helpful for us to summarize the theological and practical implications that we have seen thus far from 1 Corinthians 12:1–7.

---

22 F.F. Bruce. *The New Century Bible Commentary: I&II Corinthians.* (Grand Rapids, Eerdmans 1971).118

23 BDAG, 960.

24 Paul's statement here regarding the purpose of spiritual gifts being for the *common good* is incredibly significant when interpreting chapter 14 and understanding the point he makes regarding ecstatic utterances and the spiritual gift of tongues.

All spiritual gifts are supernaturally empowered, and therefore it is biblically inaccurate to make distinctions between the gifts listed in the Scriptures, naming some as miraculous and others as non-miraculous, or some as sign gifts and others as non-sign gifts.[25] Therefore, we must be careful not to elevate some spiritual gifts as more "spectacular gifts" than others, and therein the people to whom more "spectacular gifts" have been given as more valuable than others.[26] This appears to be the main point Paul is making in 1 Corinthians 12, especially as he writes about the body of Christ in verses 14–30.

It is difficult to determine how exactly the gifts listed in the Scriptures will be seen or experienced by others. Some gifts may indeed appear more supernatural or spectacular than others. For example, George Muller exercising the spiritual gift of faith while running an orphanage appears to be more supernatural or spectacular than a pastor working hard at preparing a sermon and exercising the gift(s) of knowledge or teaching. However, 1 Corinthians 12 states that both gifts are equally supernatural, being given and empowered by the Holy Spirit at his sole discretion.

Spiritual gifts have been given by God the Father, through God the Holy Spirit, for the building up of the body of God the Son. Believers are commanded to use the spiritual gifts they have been given, according to His will, and all the gifts are available for use as the Spirit empowers and apportions. These gifts serve as a witness to the gospel message and are distinct from signs and wonders (Heb. 2:4).

The church today should distinguish between spiritual gifts and signs and wonders so that we can accept that God has given them for the building up of the body and reject what is not from God, namely false signs and wonders. Signs and wonders, which God also used

---

25 There is no biblical explanation to support the terms sign and non-sign gifts. The application of these terms upon 1 Cor. 12 makes exegesis of Paul's list of spiritual gifts choppy and inconsistent with the other lists he makes regarding the work of the Holy Spirit (Rom. 12:3–8, Gal. 5:22–23). Furthermore, there is no place in the New Testament that the words "sign gifts" appear together.

26 A point also made by Wayne Grudem in his *Systematic Theology* book on p. 1027.

to confirm the gospel message, have ceased and were limited to the Apostles and their close associates.

Having established the source and purpose of spiritual gifts, and how they differ from others in Corinth, who may be doing demonic works, Paul now gives a list of specific gifts. It is toward a definition of the individual spiritual gifts that we turn our attention next.

PART II

Spiritual Gifts

7

WISDOM, KNOWLEDGE, AND FAITH

I must confess that my first attempt at biblically defining each gift fell woefully short of any legitimate standard of Bible interpretation! As I have already noted, in my quest for answers I found myself wanting certain things to be true (or certain definitions to be true) and merely declared that they were true without doing the hard work of understanding what the Bible says. Obviously, that's the last way to do solid interpretive work in the Scriptures.

To ensure I didn't repeat this error, I have completely rewritten that original document and this section. It looks nothing like the sermon notes I used to preach on spiritual gifts back in August 2011. Lord willing, what follows now is a much more detailed look at how each gift is defined. I will begin each section with a summary definition and after that provide greater detail and explanation as to how I arrived at each definition.

Utterance of Wisdom (λόγος σοφίας)—Those gifted with the ability to practically apply biblical knowledge.[1]

Throughout the Old Testament, wisdom is closely attached to the fear of the Lord and obedience to His revealed word.[2] Regarding wisdom in the Old Testament, and the use of wisdom in the Septuagint (LXX)[3] the TDNT states, "The translation 'wise' or 'wisdom'

---

1 BDAG, 599 "proclamation of wisdom, speaking wisely."

2 Deut. 4:6; 1 Chron. 22:12; Ps. 50:8, 110:10; Prov. 1:7, 3:4–5, 9:10, 10:23.

3 The Septuagint is the Greek translation of the Old Testament. *Septuaginta: With Morphology*. Electronic ed. Stuttgart: Deutsche Bibelgesellschaft, 1979.

is inexact; it catches neither the range nor the precise meaning of the originals, which suggest experienced and competent mastery of life and its various problems. The most common parallels have to do with perception, understanding, or skill, although parallels with uprightness and honesty are also common. The parallels show that action rather than thought is the point. In contrast, folly is a disorder that also finds expression in behavior."[4]

While it is difficult to precisely determine what Paul means by an utterance of wisdom, throughout 1 Corinthians Paul's use of the word communicates the idea of reasoned thought and understanding. Gordon Fee writes, "Thus, in the present case the 'utterance of wisdom' comes 'through the Spirit,' and in Corinth it is almost certainly to be found among those who give Spirit-inspired utterances that proclaim Christ crucified in this highly 'wisdom'-conscious community."[5]

In 1 Corinthians alone, Paul uses the word *wisdom* 17 times.[6] Through much of chapter 1, Paul's argument and his use of the word *wisdom* is against Greeks who *seek wisdom,* (v. 1:22) or those who want to know and understand things based on the *wisdom of the world* (v. 1:20).

However, Paul is not against wisdom, and it is among the mature that he imparts wisdom, though not a wisdom of this age (v. 2:6). Regarding these different types of wisdom, Paul wants the Corinthians' faith to rest, not on the wisdom of men, but in the power of God (v. 2:5).

The Greeks sought wisdom and desperately wanted all things to make sense; however, the cross is the opposite of worldly wisdom to those who are perishing (v. 1:18). Yet, rather than abandoning reasoned thought or the preaching of the Scriptures, Paul imparts a reasoned and logical explanation of who Christ is and does so from the Scriptures (vv. 15:3–5) as the Spirit interprets spiritual truths to those who are spiritual (v. 2:13).

---

4 TDNT, 1057.

5 Gordon Fee, *The First Epistle to the Corinthians* (Grand Rapids: Eerdmans, 1987), 657.

6 1:17, 19, 20, 21, 22, 24, 30; 2:1, 4, 5, 6, 7, 13; 3:19; and 12:8.

This is the same Spirit who now empowers *spiritual people* (πνευματικός)[7] to speak words of wisdom, practically applying the truth of God's Word. The church will continue to need men and women specifically gifted by the Holy Spirit to help her practically apply God's word to everyday life, and God supernaturally gifts individuals within His church to do just that.

Utterance of Knowledge (λόγος γνώσεως)—Those gifted in learning and studying the Scriptures and connecting the dots. It is the comprehension or intellectual grasp of something.[8]

Closely related to the utterance of wisdom is the utterance of knowledge. Both gifts that Paul lists have the word utterance or word (λόγος) in them, which tells us that both gifts are related to speaking or communication. The emphasis with *knowledge* appears to be on learning and studying of the Scriptures.

In 1 Corinthians Paul's use of this word is similar to how he uses the word *wisdom,* in that he contrasts a wisdom of the world, with the wisdom of God. Regarding knowledge, we see in chapter 8 that there was a claim of *knowledge,* and actions that followed, that did not benefit but rather harmed the body.

As noted earlier, Paul addresses idol worship in 1 Corinthians 8, and one of the questions he specifically addresses appears to be an issue of Christian liberty. Apparently, some believers in the Corinthian church had *knowledge* that they were free to eat food sacrificed to idols; however, this *knowledge* was making them arrogant, and their brothers and sisters were not being built up (8:1). As a result, Paul exhorts them not to sin against one another by wounding the conscience of the weak believer. Rather than exert their freedom, they are to surrender their personal rights so that a brother or sister may not stumble (8:12–13).

In contrast to their *knowledge* the Corinthians were to love one another and build one another up. Thus, we learn that there is a knowledge that puffs up and a knowledge that builds up.

---

7 The word *spiritual* in 2:13 is the same word Paul uses in 12:1 in referencing spiritual gifts/people.

8 BDAG, 203.

To Each Is Given

The spiritual gift of knowledge is not just knowing true things. It is the Spirit-empowered ability to teach and apply the word of God so that the people of God are strengthened and built up.

John MacArthur provides a helpful description of this gift saying, "The gifted person is supernaturally enabled not only to discover truths from the facts of the Scripture but to explain and interpret those truths in order to help others understand them."[9] Those with the gift of knowledge are empowered by the Spirit to understand God's Word, connecting the dots from Genesis to Revelation.

Faith (πίστις)—Those gifted with the ability to trust God and remind God's people never to forget who He is and what He has promised even in the most difficult of human circumstances. It is "an unquestioning belief in God's power to aid people with miracles, the faith that 'moves mountains'" (1 Cor. 13:2).[10]

The Apostle Paul uses the word *faith* 142 times throughout his letters and, with the exception of Romans 3:3, the word *faith* speaks of a believer's trust or belief in God.[11] While the context regarding Paul's use of the word does shift between saving faith and sustaining or living faith, he consistently points to the triune God as the one whom believers put their faith in. Garland helpfully and simply defines this gift as an "internal trust in God, [that] results in external results."[12]

As a result, we must be careful not to conclude that the *gift of faith* includes hopeful thinking, good vibes, or perhaps well wishes from a kind someone we may know or meet. On the contrary, the *gift of faith* is solely rooted in the sovereignty of God and focuses completely on Him.

Furthermore, because this is a gift that some have been given by the Spirit, we must also be careful not to conclude that the spiritual gift of *faith* is the gift of saving faith. Saving faith is indeed a gift, as Paul communicates in Ephesians 2:8, and all believers have been given that gift. However, the spiritual gift of *faith* is different in that

---

9 MacArthur, *1 Corinthians*, 299.

10 BDAG, 820.

11 In Romans 3:3 Paul uses the word πίστιν to write about the *faithfulness of God*.

12 David Garland, *1 Corinthians* (Grand Rapids: Baker Academic, 2003) 581.

it is given only to some believers so that the body of Christ may be built up and strengthened. Nevertheless, even if this is not one's gift, all believers are commanded to live by faith (Rom. 1:17).[13]

Those with the gift of faith believe that if God is for them no one can be against them. However, this gift is not a blank check to make God serve us in whatever ways we desire. We must remember that this gift is apportioned individually as He wills, and empowered as He wills. Positively stated, those with this gift exhort and encourage everyone to consider God, seek Him passionately, trust in His promises, and believe that in the end what He does will be good.

---

13 Similarly, all believers are commanded to be generous and merciful while some are supernaturally gifted to do so.

8
HEALINGS AND MIRACLES

Gifts of Healings (χαρίσματα ἰαμάτων)—Those gifted by the Holy Spirit to heal.[1]

Like the gift of faith, we must again acknowledge that gifts of healings are given and empowered according to the will of the Holy Spirit. However, among the groups who believe that this gift is still given to the church today, there exists a serious disagreement regarding whether physical healing is guaranteed or not.

This was vividly illustrated one morning by a fellow pastor I met for coffee. The purpose of our meeting was to discuss spiritual gifts and what his church believed regarding them. As we discussed the various gifts and how he has seen them work, he began to lament that he once witnessed a gentleman in a "healing line" die right before being prayed for. My friend grieved that this man was only two people away from being prayed for and receiving his healing. As we continued to discuss this tragic scene it increasingly became clear that my friend's view of this spiritual gift was that it guaranteed healing if the person could only have been prayed for by the healer. Specifically, he quoted Matthew 8:16–17, "That evening they brought to him many who were oppressed by demons, and he cast out the spirits with a word and healed all who were sick. This was to fulfill what was spoken by the prophet Isaiah: 'He took our illnesses and bore our diseases.' "

In short, my friend told me that healing "is guaranteed in the atonement." To state my friend's definition another way, he believes the gift of healing is not empowered or apportioned by the Holy Spirit

---

1 BDAG, 464.

as He wills, rather, it is empowered and apportioned by the Holy Spirit at all times because it is always God's will to heal, and He guarantees physical healing in the atonement.

Without question, the debate regarding gifts of healings is also a debate about the theology that informs the interpretation of this gift. I know of no one who denies God's ability to heal the sick today as Jesus did when he walked the earth. Even those who believe this gift is not for the church today still acknowledge that God can heal physically anytime He wants. The debate is centered around whether God *must* heal, not whether God *can* heal.

Healing *is* guaranteed in the atonement of Jesus Christ! However, *when* that healing happens is not guaranteed.[2] One day, every believer in Jesus Christ will be forever and eternally united with Him and will no longer suffer from sin, sickness, death, crying, pain, or mourning because these former things will have passed away (Rev. 21:4).

While this gift is for the church today, there is no guarantee that a healing will occur exactly as prayed for. Healing occurs according to God's will, not our wills; nor through our use of the right words to create a pseudo-incantation that forces God's hand.

Prominent signs and wonders leader, Bill Johnson, answers the question, "Is it always God's will to heal?" with a question of his own. Johnson writes, "How can God choose not to heal someone when He already purchased their healing?"[3] Johnson, alongside many others, teaches that physical healing is guaranteed and that if healing does not occur, the afflicted person did not have enough faith to "call their healing in."[4] Tragically, this understanding of

---

2 To this point, we must note that every person who is living today will one day die. To say that physical healing is guaranteed here and now ignores that death as a curse of the fall is still very much a part of the human experience.

3 Johnson, "Always God's Will to Heal? " n.d. http:// bjm.org/qa/is-it-always-gods-will-to-heal-someone/ - ch.1, n.14

4 This is the exact phrase my pastor friend used to describe how one appropriates their healing. He likened healing to owning a dog that has run out into the field behind your house. You have to "call the dog in" if you want the dog to come home, but you already own the dog. As to healing, the healing is already ours. What is left is our calling the healing into existence and claiming it for ourselves.

Scripture is not only off base, but it also demoralizes the faith of the one who is suffering.[5]

Furthermore, Scripture is clear that God ordains and uses suffering in our lives for his glory and our good. While a full theology of suffering is outside the scope of this book, the following passages speak clearly to God's plan for, and use of, suffering in our lives.

Romans 8:18–25

"For I consider that the sufferings of this present time are not worth comparing with the glory that is to be revealed to us. For the creation waits with eager longing for the revealing of the sons of God. For the creation was subjected to futility, not willingly, but because of him who subjected it, in hope that the creation itself will be set free from its bondage to corruption and obtain the freedom of the glory of the children of God. For we know that the whole creation has been groaning together in the pains of childbirth until now. And not only the creation, but we ourselves, who have the first fruits of the Spirit, groan inwardly as we wait eagerly for adoption as sons, the redemption of our bodies. For in this hope we were saved. Now hope that is seen is not hope. For who hopes for what he sees? But if we hope for what we do not see, we wait for it with patience."

Philippians 1:29–30

"For it has been granted to you that for the sake of Christ you should not only believe in him but also suffer for his sake, engaged in the same conflict that you saw I had and now hear that I still have."

1 Thessalonians 3:1–4

"Therefore, when we could bear it no longer, we were willing to be left behind at Athens alone, and we sent Timothy, our brother and God's coworker in the gospel of Christ, to establish and exhort you in your faith, that no one be moved by these afflictions. For you yourselves know that we are destined for this. For when we were with you,

---

5 Anecdotally countering this point is the observation that many of the individuals who teach this theology wear eyeglasses! I have always found it humorous that the very people who speak of guaranteed healing have not experienced healing in their own eyesight.

we kept telling you beforehand that we were to suffer affliction, just as it has come to pass, and just as you know."

James 1:2–4
"Count it all joy, my brothers, when you meet trials of various kinds, for you know that the testing of your faith produces steadfastness. And let steadfastness have its full effect, that you may be perfect and complete, lacking in nothing."

Hebrews 11:36–40
"Others suffered mocking and flogging, and even chains and imprisonment. They were stoned, they were sawn in two, they were killed with the sword. They went about in skins of sheep and goats, destitute, afflicted, mistreated—of whom the world was not worthy—wandering about in deserts and mountains, and in dens and caves of the earth.

And all these, though commended through their faith, did not receive what was promised, since God had provided something better for us, that apart from us they should not be made perfect."

2 Corinthians 4:16–5:10
"So we do not lose heart. Though our outer self is wasting away, our inner self is being renewed day by day. For this light momentary affliction is preparing for us an eternal weight of glory beyond all comparison, as we look not to the things that are seen but to the things that are unseen. For the things that are seen are transient, but the things that are unseen are eternal.

For we know that if the tent that is our earthly home is destroyed, we have a building from God, a house not made with hands, eternal in the heavens. For in this tent we groan, longing to put on our heavenly dwelling, if indeed by putting it on we may not be found naked. For while we are still in this tent, we groan, being burdened—not that we would be unclothed, but that we would be further clothed, so that what is mortal may be swallowed up by life. He who has prepared us for this very thing is God, who has given us the Spirit as a guarantee.

So we are always of good courage. We know that while we are at home in the body we are away from the Lord, for we walk by faith, not by sight. Yes, we are of good courage, and we would rather be away from the body and at home with the Lord. So whether we are at home or away, we make it our aim to please him. For we must all appear before the judgment seat of Christ, so that each one may receive what is due for what he has done in the body, whether good or evil."

1 Peter 1:6–9

"In this you rejoice, though now for a little while, if necessary, you have been grieved by various trials, so that the tested genuineness of your faith—more precious than gold that perishes though it is tested by fire—may be found to result in praise and glory and honor at the revelation of Jesus Christ. Though you have not seen him, you love him. Though you do not now see him, you believe in him and rejoice with joy that is inexpressible and filled with glory, obtaining the outcome of your faith, the salvation of your souls."

Returning to the *gifts of healings* that Paul lists in 1 Corinthians 12, we must make a few observations. First, the presence of the two plurals.[6] Both *gift* and *healing* are in the plural. Because of this double plural we should not conclude that there is a singular gift of healing or a singular way that healing is brought about. It may be God's will to heal immediately when someone is prayed for, or it may be His will to heal through medicine or surgery. It may also be God's will to sustain the individual through their suffering (James 1:2–4, 2 Cor. 12:1–10).

Secondly, we must not forget that the distribution and empowerment of these gifts is at the will of the Holy Spirit. Believers are not little gods, and they do not possess a power within themselves to command a healing. However, believers should pray boldly for one another that God would heal! Those who are afflicted should call for the elders to pray and anoint them with oil (James 5:14–15).[7]

---

6 This occurs all three times Paul lists this gift in 1 Corinthians 12.

7 When my elder team and I pray and anoint someone we pray specifically for three things: for God to give the grace of immediate healing; for God to give the grace of healing through medicine; for God to give his sustaining grace if He chooses to not heal and that the ailing person may grow in their faith as they walk through this trial.

We live in a broken and fallen world, and when we see friends suffering with affliction or families lose children to disease, we should rightly groan under the weight of sin that so deeply affects every aspect of life. It is also right to boldly pray for full and complete healing and groan when God does not choose to heal as we prayed because the consequence of Adam's sin has deeply marred God's very good creation.

However, we must also rejoice that Christ has conquered sin and has risen from the grave and that he has told us, "today's light and momentary affliction is preparing for us an eternal weight of glory beyond all comparison" (2 Cor. 4:17). This world is not the best that there will ever be. God has something far greater in store for those who have trusted in Jesus Christ by grace through faith.

Working of Miracles (ἐνεργήματα δυνάμεων)—Those gifted to call on God to show up and do miraculous things. BDAG defines this as "a deed that exhibits ability to function powerfully." [8]

Like *gifts of healings*, this spiritual gift is also written with two plurals. It can be translated as the *workings of miracles*. Consequently, as was concluded with *gifts of healings*, we should not think of one kind of working or miracle. The language Paul uses is specifically indicating a plurality.

In the church today, we should be bold in asking God to do the miraculous and yet cautious that our requests are ultimately for His glory and not our own. As with the gift of faith, and gifts and healings, we must remind ourselves that the working of miracles is apportioned and empowered by the Spirit as He wills, not as we will. Believers must not lose focus on God's sovereignty regarding the distribution and use of this gift. To do so again errs in teaching that we are little gods capable of commanding the winds and the waves as we wish.

---

8 BDAG, 263.

9

PROPHECY AND
DISCERNING THE SPIRITS

Prophecy (προφητεία)—Those gifted to proclaim and explain God's Word,[1] and at times receive spontaneous insights (regarding the explanation and application of God's Word) from the Holy Spirit.

This gift, like the gifts of healings and workings of miracles, is hotly debated because of significant differences in how this gift is defined. Leaders within the NAR movement, "teach that New Testament prophets do have the same level of authority as Old Testament Prophets and that they do hold a formal governing office."[2] Given that the Old Testament office of Prophet was a revelatory office that God used to speak His Words to His people we should be cautious regarding any claim that people today speak new revelation for God as the Old Testament Prophets did.

To be fair to NAR leaders, Peter Wagner does indicate that the canon of Scripture "cannot be added to or subtracted from."[3] However, we are left to wonder what level of authority these new revelations carry with them, if they are to be perfect as Old Testament prophecies were, and to what degree they are to be obeyed. Old Testament Prophets were held to the standard of absolute perfection in their prophecies because they were revealing God's Word to His people (Deut. 18:20-22). As such, those who did not obey the Prophets were disciplined and punished since the Prophets spoke for God.

---

1 BDAG, 889.

2 R. Douglas Geivett and Holly Pivec, *God's Super-Apostles: Encountering the Worldwide Prophets and Apostles Movement* (Wooster: Weaver Publishing, 2014), 71.

3 Wagner, *Apostles,* 34.

To Each Is Given

Wagner also contends that apostles receive revelation directly from God. He writes, "Revelation from God is communicated to apostles in two ways. One method is when the apostle, like the Apostle Paul, receives the revelation directly.... God can and does reveal His plans directly to apostles. But He also reveals, His plans to prophets who, in turn, communicate them to apostles." [4] Conversely, continuationists and cessationists believe that the canon of Scripture is closed, and God is no longer giving inspired revelation to Apostles and Prophets.

The differences could not be any starker, nor the stakes any higher. If God is still revealing Scripture through governing Prophets today, who have Old Testament authority, then those who reject their prophetic messages are rejecting the Word of God.[5] However, if God is not revealing new Scripture, then those claiming Scripture level authority and new revelations must be rejected as false prophets.

The word translated *prophecy* (προφητεία) in 1 Corinthians 12:10 is a noun and occurs 19 times throughout the New Testament. It is used once by Matthew,[6] nine times by Paul,[7] twice by Peter,[8] and seven times by the Apostle John.[9] As noted earlier, BDAG defines this word as "the gift of interpreting divine will or purpose."[10]

---

4 Ibid. 34, 37. It is difficult to know exactly what Wagner means when he uses the word *revelation*. In one paragraph he rightly acknowledges that the canon "cannot be added to or subtracted from," and we are left to conclude that this new revelation is not equal in authority to Scripture. However, two paragraphs later he writes that apostles today receive revelation "like the apostle Paul" which would seem to place these new revelations on a level equal in authority to Scripture.

5 In his book, *The Gift of Prophecy*, Wayne Grudem convincingly identifies the Old Testament Prophets and the New Testament Apostle together, thus indicating there are not modern day (or First Century) Prophets like there were in the Old Testament. Regarding the similarities of these two offices he writes, "The most significant parallel between Old Testament prophets and New Testament apostles, however, is the ability to write words of Scripture, words that have absolute divine authority" (p. 29).

6 Matt. 13:14.

7 Rom. 12:6; 1 Cor. 12:10, 13:2, 13:8, 14:6, 14:22; 1 Thess. 5:20; 1 Tim. 1:18, 4:14.

8 2 Peter 1:20, 1:21.

9 Rev. 1:3, 11:6, 19:10, 22:7, 22:10, 22:18, 22:19.

10 BDAG, 889.

The verbal form of this word occurs 28 times in the New Testament and generally refers to the act of speaking.[11] Specifically, it is used to refer to the content, or message spoken, not the person speaking.[12]

When looking at the specific instances that *prophecy* is used in the New Testament (both noun and verb form) it is important to note exactly what this word is referring to. From the passages in which these two words are used we can observe two categories: (1) a specific reference to inspired Scripture, (2) a reference to a non-Scripture message.[13] By categorizing these instances of *prophecy,* we find greater clarity in what the Apostle Paul is referring to in 1 Corinthians 12 and Romans 12.

In my opinion, while *prophecy* is used in the New Testament to refer specifically to inspired Scripture, the Apostle Paul never uses *prophecy* in this way. Rather, he uses this word exclusively in reference to non-Scripture messages that do not have a Scripture level of authority. Paul is not intending to communicate that new Scripture is being given by God, he is communicating that God is giving insight into his word to further our understanding and application.[14] It is in this sense that he uses the word *revelation* in 1 Corinthians 14:26, 30.

Passages such as 1 Corinthians 14:31 further help us understand that Paul is not referring to the new revelation of Scripture, but to the proclamation and application of Scripture. Paul writes, "For you can all prophesy one by one, so that all may learn and all be en-

---

11 Matt. 7:22, 11:13, 15:7, 26:68; Mark 7:6, 14:65; Luke 1:67, 22:64; John 11:51; Acts 2:17, 18, 19:6, 21:9; 1 Cor. 11:4, 11:5, 13:9, 14:1, 14:3, 14:4, 14:5 (twice), 14:24, 14:31, 14:3; 1 Peter 1:10; Jude 14; Rev. 10:11, 11:3.

12 In the NT the noun *Prophet* refers to the one speaking rather than the message being spoken and occurs 144 times.

13 See Appendix A for a table that breaks down the occurrences of *prophecy* into these two categories.

14 In non-charismatic churches we see this gift often described as and prefaced with "the Lord laid it on my heart." The person sharing believes that God has instructed to them to share something with someone. Usually it is a Scripture passage that is shared, though it may be something more specific to apply the Scriptures to a certain situation. These instances are best received with caution so that they may be tested against God's Word.

couraged...." Regarding this passage, Grudem comments that "The emphasis of the prophecy would have been on immediate practical application to the hearers' lives."[15] Specifically, Paul wants the church to be built up and encouraged (v. 14:3), and to this end five mindful words of prophecy are exceedingly more valuable than 10,000 mindless words spoken in a tongue that no one can understand (v. 14:9).

At the beginning of 1 Corinthians 14, Paul commanded his audience to "earnestly desire (ζηλοῦτε) the spiritual gifts, especially that you may prophesy." In verse 31, he not only reaffirms his desire for those in this church to prophesy but again communicates what the purpose of such prophecy is. They are all (πάντες) to prophesy for the purpose (ἵνα) of the entire (πάντες) church's benefit. Or, to say it another way, all are to prophecy so that all may learn and be encouraged.

Unfortunately, we do not know what type of prophecies occurred in the Corinthian church after they received Paul's letter and instruction.[16] Perhaps they included specific and practical ways to apply Paul's letter or faithful ways to interpret and apply the Old Testament; we simply do not know. We do know that Paul commands the church in Corinth to earnestly desire the gift of prophecy and gives them instructions for its use in their worship services. Yet, while doing so he never equates their use of this gift to a level of authority equal to Scripture.

Practically speaking, we should see this gift as essential to the life and health of local churches and individual believers. We also must earnestly desire this gift so that the church may be built up, instructed, and encouraged.

The gift of prophecy is the ability to proclaim and explain God's Word and, at times, receive spontaneous insights regarding the explanation and application of God's Word from the Holy Spirit. The point of this gift is not to foretell the future or make baseless promises about good health, future wealth, or even the end of the world. The

---

15 Wayne Grudem, *The Gift of Prophecy* (Wheaton: Crossway, 2000), 129.

16 Or in Thessalonica. Paul instructs them to "not despise prophecies," 1 Thess. 5:20.

point of this gift is to proclaim and explain God's Word so that His body is built up, instructed, and encouraged.

Regarding "spontaneous insights," it is entirely possible the Holy Spirit may give someone a point of application while preaching or counseling that he had not thought of during his preparation. The prompting of the Holy Spirit to share something specific that was unplanned may help explain God's Word to those listening in ways they would not have otherwise understood.

Also, the Holy Spirit may give a point of explanation or application to someone while studying and reading God's Word that may help a fellow believer with something they are experiencing in life. Allowing for the Holy Spirit to spontaneously suggest a point of explanation or application of the Scriptures recognizes the work of the Holy Spirit to illuminate the Word of God and God's desire that his Word be known, understood, and obeyed.

Before we move on, one further point is necessary. The presence and use of this gift does not in any way diminish or minimize the significance of, or need for, sound Bible interpretation skills. God *may* give spontaneous insights regarding the explanation and application of a text; however, we must always be diligent to study and *rightly divide the word of truth* (2 Tim. 2:15).

Paul further instructs Timothy, and by extension us, in 2 Timothy 4:3–4 that "that time is coming when people will not endure sound teaching, but having itching ears they will accumulate for themselves teachers to suit their own passions, and will turn away from listening to the truth and wander off into silly myths." Tragically, this is happening all too often today across churches of all denominations and affiliations.

Furthermore, we have something *more sure* (2 Pet. 1:19) than the greatest spiritual experiences or spontaneous insights. We have the Word of God and we must always keep His Word as the final authority for our lives.

We must be people who study, learn, pray, and seek to understand what God has already said. We must cling to His Word, for His Word is enough! We do not need fancy, out-of-context interpretations and applications of the Scriptures. We need only to understand what God has said and how it applies to our lives.

Discerning the Spirits (διακρίσεις πνευμάτων)—Those gifted with the supernatural "ability to distinguish and evaluate" between false spirits and the Holy Spirit; between what is true, and what is false.[17]

As noted in chapter six, the context of 1 Corinthians 12 begins with Paul answering questions regarding *spiritual people*. This church struggled to see a differentiation between people who may have *appeared* spiritual, performing supernatural acts, while claiming, "Jesus is accursed." In answering these questions, Paul gives the entire church instructions on how to evaluate these very public occurrences, and he also indicates there is a supernatural gifting of the Holy Spirit that helps distinguish truth from falsehood.

Regarding this gift Carson writes, "There is ever a need to distinguish demonic forces from the Holy Spirit. This gift is apparently designed to meet that need. The insight needed may be granted by some special enduement; or, if 1 John 4:1–6 is anything to go by, the outworking of this gift may on occasion be the by-product of profound doctrinal discernment."[18]

MacArthur helpfully adds, "those with the gift of discernment are the Holy Spirit's inspectors, His counterfeit experts to whom He gives special insight and understanding."[19] Because absolute truth is central to the Christian faith, and the purity of the gospel, God has given people within His church the special ability to discern truth from error.

In my experience, those with this gift are often misunderstood and, while they are confident in what they see theologically, they feel a bit like the village idiot because they are often the only ones who initially see an error. Those with this gift are often the first to say no to the

---

17 BDAG, 231.

18 Carson, *Showing the Spirit*, 40.

19 MacArthur, *1 Corinthians*, 304.

latest and greatest bands or books, and the church at large doesn't understand them. The purpose of this gift not only includes deciphering information but warning and alerting other believers of errors. At times this gift positions them against the Christian subculture because they "connect theological dots" before anyone else, and they can often be dismissed and pushed aside.

As we move toward the last two gifts that Paul mentions, we must pause to note that tongues and the interpretation of tongues are perhaps the two most controversial gifts within the entire list. Given what Paul writes in 1 Corinthians 14, it appears that even the church in Corinth had a difficult time accurately understanding what tongues are, what they are not, and what their purpose is. For our purposes, we will first look at the interpretation of tongues and then secondly, in much greater detail, the gift of tongues.

10

TONGUES AND THE INTERPRETATION THEREOF

To say that the spiritual gifts of tongues has been a significant point of widespread disagreement is an understatement of gargantuan proportions! A good number of non-Pentecostal and charismatic churches practice the *gift of tongues* within their worship services as part of their normal corporate gatherings. Pentecostal churches teach that tongues are a confirmation of the baptism of the Holy Spirit.[1] In contrast to these positions and practices, many other churches and church leaders claim that the gift of tongues, and therefore the interpretation thereof, ceased with the completion of the canon.

Within the Charis Fellowship, there is little public discussion about the spiritual gift of tongues. Because of the theological convictions our Fellowship shares, I believe we would find ourselves somewhere in the middle of the theological pack; certainly, some churches and pastors believe that these gifts have ceased while others believe they are still for today.

As I've contended thus far, all the gifts of the Spirit are still for today, and the church must pursue these gifts. However, spiritual gifts are not signs and wonders, and while there is similarity, they each serve a different purpose.

As we saw in chapter six, the purpose of spiritual gifts is to bear witness to the gospel and for the building up of the body. The purpose of signs and wonders was to authenticate both the message (of the gospel) and the messenger.

---

1 See definitions in chapter 1.

To Each Is Given

How then are we to define the gifts of tongues and interpretation of tongues? And can a definition be reached that is faithful to what the Scriptures reveal about spiritual gifts and the baptizing, filling, and indwelling work of the Holy Spirit? We turn our attention to these matters next.

Interpretation of Tongues (ἑρμηνεία γλωσσῶν)—The Spirit-empowered ability to interpret the speaking of a known language that is unknown to the interpreter.

The word *interpretation* (ἑρμηνεία) is defined as the "capacity of doing translation" and appears only twice in the entire New Testament (1 Cor.12:10 and 1 Cor. 14:26).[2] In both passages, Paul is concerned that the hearers understand what has been said.

To this end, the interpretation of tongues had an important function in the Corinthian church. The church could not benefit if a language were spoken that could not be translated or understood. Consequently, if any had a message in *tongues* from the Lord this message was to be interpreted so that it could be understood, and if there is no one interpreting there should be no one speaking.

Before we consider how else we may practically see this gift in operation today, we must understand what tongues are. By understanding what Paul identifies as the gift of tongues, we will better understand how the gift of interpretation fits in the life of the church.

Kinds of Tongues (γένη γλωσσῶν)—The Spirit-empowered ability to speak in a known language that is unknown to the speaker, for the purpose of proclaiming the gospel. Part of the challenge in defining this gift lies with how the word *tongue* (γλωσσα) is used throughout the New Testament. BDAG notes three distinct possibilities for the use of this word: (1) "organ of speech," (2) "distinctive language," and (3) "ecstatic utterances."[3]

The most common use of tongues is to describe the speaking of existing world languages. There are also numerous instances when this

---

2 BDAG, 393.
3 BDAG, 201.

word is used to describe the tongue as a body part and not the speaking of languages, whether known or unintelligible. Notably, Paul is the only biblical author to use *tongues* when referring to ecstatic utterances and does so five times.

Here is a breakdown of the New Testament occurrences of *tongues*. Admittedly, the categorizing of these passages into these three categories (particularly the category of utterances) reflects my interpretation of these passages and is not an interpretation held by everyone.

Body Part	Languages	Utterances
Mark 7:33 (s) [4]		
Mark 7:35 (s)		
	Mark 16:17 (p)	
Luke 1:64 (s)		
Luke 16:24 (s)		
	Acts 2:3 (p)	
	Acts 2:4 (p)	
	Acts 2:11 (p)	
Acts 2:26 (s)		
	Acts 10:46 (p)	
	Acts 19:6 (p)	
Romans 3:13 (p)		

---

4 (s) for singular, (p) for plural.

To Each Is Given

Body Part	Languages	Utterances
Romans 4:11 (s)		
	1 Corinthians 12:10 (p) x2	
	1 Corinthians 12:28 (p)	
	1 Corinthians 12:30 (p)	
	1 Corinthians 13:1 (p)	
	1 Corinthians 13:8 (p)	
		1 Corinthians 14:2 (s)
		1 Corinthians 14:4 (s)
	1 Corinthians 14:5 (p) x2	
	1 Corinthians 14:6 (p)	
1 Corinthians 14:9 (s)		
		1 Corinthians 14:13 (s) x2
		1 Corinthians 14:14 (s)
	1 Corinthians 14:18 (p)	
		1 Corinthians 14:19 (s)
	1 Corinthians 14:22 (p)	
	1 Corinthians 14:23 (p)	
		1 Corinthians 14:26 (s)

Body Part	Languages	Utterances
	1 Corinthians 14:27 (s)	
	1 Corinthians 14:39 (p)	
Philippians 2:11 (s)		
James 1:26 (s)		
James 3:5 (s)		
James 3:6 (s) x2		
James 3:8 (s)		
1 Peter 3:10 (s)		
1 John 3:18 (s)		
	Revelation 5:9 (s)	
	Revelation 7:9 (p)	
	Revelation 10:11 (p)	
	Revelation 11:9 (p)	
	Revelation 13:7 (s)	
	Revelation 14:6 (s)	
Revelation 16:10 (p)		
	Revelation 17:15 (p)	

Table 1

To Each Is Given

Regarding this breakdown, we can make a few general observations:

- All things considered, the word *tongue(s)* is not frequently used in the New Testament, occurring only 50 times by six biblical authors.
- James and Peter only use the word *tongue(s)* to refer to a body part.
- Mark, Luke, Paul, and John use the word *tongue(s)* in at least two ways.
- Paul is the only biblical author to use the word *tongue(s)* to refer to speech that is not intelligible.[5]

What emerges from this analysis is that tongues does not have one consistent usage or definition within the New Testament. As a result, we need to concentrate on the passages in which tongues is used to refer to a work of the Spirit and not merely language spoken by people or the part of our bodies.

---

5 1 Corinthians 14:2, 9, 13, 14, 19, 26.

11

TONGUES IN THE BOOK OF ACTS

Before looking specifically at 1 Corinthians 12–14, it will be helpful to consider what Luke writes regarding the speaking of tongues in the book of Acts. The primary focus of our attention will be the events of Pentecost as recorded in Acts 2, for there we see the spiritual gift of tongues on full display. Furthermore, I believe that Paul's explanation of tongues in 1 Corinthians 14:22–40 fits exactly with what happened at Pentecost—giving us a real-life example of how the Holy Spirit may apportion and empower this gift.[1]

Luke records in Acts 2,

> "When the day of Pentecost arrived, they were all together in one place. And suddenly there came from heaven a sound like a mighty rushing wind, and it filled the entire house where they were sitting. And divided tongues as of fire appeared to them and rested on each one of them. And they

---

[1] Before proceeding, I must note that in large regard, I base my definition of tongues on what happened in Acts 2. I do so because Acts 2 is chronologically before Paul's letter to the church in Corinth and the events of Acts 2 are specifically referenced in Acts 10 by Peter and "the believers from among the circumcised" (Acts 10:45). In contrast to this interpretation, a good friend of mine, who is also a pastor within the Charis Fellowship, defines tongues in Acts 2 from 1 Cor. 12–14 because the book of 1 Corinthians was written by Paul before Luke wrote the book of Acts. His argument is also based on chronology! Specifically, he contends that when Luke wrote Acts 2 he had the events of Corinth and Paul's instructions to the Corinthians in mind. I disagree with his approach but desire to be gracious to those who may hold such a view while being transparent regarding the approach I take when defining this gift.

> were all filled with the Holy Spirit and began to speak in other tongues as the Spirit gave them utterance."
>
> Now there were dwelling in Jerusalem Jews, devout men from every nation under heaven. And at this sound the multitude came together, and they were bewildered, because each one was hearing them speak in his own language. And they were amazed and astonished, saying, 'Are not all these who are speaking Galileans? And how is it that we hear, each of us in his own native language? Parthians and Medes and Elamites and residents of Mesopotamia, Judea and Cappadocia, Pontus and Asia, Phrygia and Pamphylia, Egypt and the parts of Libya belonging to Cyrene, and visitors from Rome, both Jews and proselytes, Cretans and Arabians—we hear them telling in our own tongues the mighty works of God.' And all were amazed and perplexed, saying to one another, 'What does this mean?' But others mocking said, 'They are filled with new wine.' "

One of the first questions we should ask in interpreting this passage is who the *they* are that were all together in one place (v.1). Was it just the 12 Apostles (now with Matthias) or was it *the company of persons* that was about 120? To determine how to interpret the *they* we must look at the entire context of chapter 1 and therefore, understand who was speaking in tongues.

In Acts 1:1–11, Luke indicates that the group is just the 11 Apostles. In Acts 1:2 Luke writes about the "day when he [Jesus] was taken up, after he had given commands through the Holy Spirit to the apostles whom he had chosen." The pronoun *them* as seen throughout verses 1–11 refers to the 11. This is further confirmed by how the two men in white robes address those who just watched Jesus ascend, calling them "Men of Galilee."

Verse 12 functions as a transition, indicating what these "men of Galilee" did in returning to Jerusalem. In verse 14, Luke tells us that more than just the 11 Apostles were in the upper room. With these men were "the women, Mary the mother of Jesus, and his brothers." Furthermore, in verse 15, we are told that the entire company of persons in this upper room "was in all about 120." Alva J. McClain writes about those in this room saying, "these were the first believers."[2] It is before this entire group that Peter stands up and speaks, declaring that they should replace Judas.

Throughout the rest of chapter 1, we are given the details regarding how Matthias was chosen to replace Judas, and what qualifications he had to meet even to be considered an Apostle. After the lots had been cast, and Matthias was identified, "he was numbered with the eleven apostles" (v. 1:26).

When we arrive at the beginning of Acts 2, Luke has already told us, "they were all together in one place." Interpreting *they* as a reference to the entire group makes the most sense contextually because beginning in verse 14 Luke indicates who some of the well-known individuals in the room were and in verse 15 tells us how large the group was.

That non-apostles, which included women, were filled with the Holy Spirit and spoke in tongues is confirmed by Peter's quotation of the prophet Joel where Joel prophesies about the Spirit being poured out on all. Peter quotes, "I will pour out my Spirit on all flesh, and your sons and daughters shall prophesy" (Acts 2:17). Part of the astonishing nature of this moment was that it was not just the 12 Apostles who were filled with the Holy Spirit and spoke in tongues. It was everyone!

Regarding the filling of the Holy Spirit and their speaking in tongues, Luke tells us in Acts 2:3 that "divided tongues as of fire appeared to them and rested on each one of them." The entire group heard the sound from heaven, saw the divided tongues of fire, and was filled with the Holy Spirit; speaking in tongues as given utterance, or as the Spirit caused them to speak boldly and loudly.[3] God was about

---

2 Alva J. McClain, *The Greatness of the Kingdom,* (Chicago: Moody Press., 1968), 398.

3 BDAG, 125.

to move in a powerful way, and He was using His disciples, men and women equally, as His ambassadors!

Luke's definition of this experience of tongues includes two important details: (1) speaking in *tongues* is an act of speaking, and (2) the speaker speaks a known language that is unknown to them. In verse 6, we are told that the devout men were bewildered "because each one was hearing them speak in his own language." The verb *speak* (λαλέω) is defined as "to make a sound, or to utter words."[4]

When interpreting *tongues* in Acts 2 as ecstatic utterances, some specifically assert that the word *speak* means to babble. However, in doing so they ignore the semantic range of this word and its use elsewhere in Scripture.[5] *Speak* is not used exclusively this way and therefore we should not immediately conclude that the tongues spoken in Acts 2 were unintelligible noises.

For example, Matthew writes that "While he [Jesus] was saying these things to them, behold, a ruler came" (Matt. 9:18). The word Matthew uses to describe the action of Jesus speaking is the same word Luke uses in Acts 2. Certainly, we would not assert that Jesus babbled to those listening to him, uttering unintelligible words that were miraculously heard and understood by those listening. To make such a conclusion forces one to interpret the miracle in Acts 2 as a miracle of hearing on the part of the unbelievers at Pentecost rather than a miracle of speaking.

In Acts 2, Luke indicates real languages were spoken by people who did not know these languages. Evidence of this is found in that native language speakers heard them speak in their own language. Homer Kent Jr. agrees and states, "The speakers used languages not hitherto known by them but perfectly understood by the hearers."[6] The Holy Spirit did not fill the unbelievers who were gathered to-

---

4 Ibid., 582.

5 Contra Smith who asserts that λαλέω is used to show that "tongues were ecstatic utterances, mostly unintelligible, and not rational expressions" in Charles Smith, *Tongues in Biblical Perspective* (Winona Lake: BHM Books 1976), 36.

6 Homer Kent, Jr., *Studies in Acts* (Winona Lake: BHM Books, 1978), 24.

gether with the spiritual gift of interpretation, he filled the believers gathered in the upper room to speak in tongues.

Not only did the 120 speak, but they also spoke in a known language. Luke also records for us in verse 6 that those gathered at Pentecost heard them "in his own language." This is the second point of the definition that emerges from what Luke records, and this is greatly instructive for us because it further defines what type of speech this was.

The word *language* (διάλεκτος) is defined by BDAG as the "language of a nation or a region."[7] Luke is the only author who uses this word in Scripture, and he does so six times.[8] Outside of Acts 2, each time Luke uses this word he indicates a real, known language.

As a result, to claim that Luke means an unknown language or gibberish in Acts 2 would be nonsensical given the way he specifically uses the term elsewhere within the same book. Plainly, Luke tells us in Acts 2:6 that the disciples spoke in tongues. These tongues were real languages, and these languages were understood by those who heard.[9]

Luke also tells us the content of their speech! In 2:11, he records that "both Jews and proselytes, Cretans and Arabians—we hear them telling in our own tongues the mighty works of God." These Jewish unbelievers from *every nation* were hearing the disciples speak the mighty works of God! Furthermore, in verse 11, we not only have the content of what was said, Luke again gives definition to how the "mighty works of God" were spoken, namely "telling in our own tongues."

To conclude that Luke intends for us to understand the tongues spoken in 2:4 are ecstatic utterances and not known languages unknown to the speaker means that we must ignore the way he uses the word

---

7 BDAG, 232.

8 Acts 1:19, 2:6, 8, 21:40, 22:2, 26:14.

9 Parthians, Medes, Elamites, residents of Mesopotamia, Judea, Cappadocia, Pontus, Asia, Phrygia, Pamphylia, Egypt, parts of Libya belonging to Cyrene, visitors from Rome, Cretans and Arabians (Acts. 2:9–11).

language elsewhere in Acts and conclude that the phrase *own tongues* in 2:11 doesn't really mean own tongues. In doing so, we must then conclude that the miracle at Pentecost was a miracle of unbelievers being empowered by the Holy Spirit to hear, not one of believers being empowered by the Holy Spirit to speak.

This would also mean that those who comment about what they hear in Acts 2:11 only *think* they are hearing the mighty works of God proclaimed in their own tongues, but what they are hearing is gibberish that the Holy Spirit is supernaturally interpreting for them.

A sounder interpretation of this event is that the tongues spoken in Acts 2 were real languages, and the amazed astonishment of those at Pentecost was not due to hearing gibberish that they understood to be the mighty works of God, but due to Galileans speaking known languages from every nation.[10] F.F. Bruce writes of those visiting Jerusalem,

> "Many of them were astonished as they heard the loud praises of God uttered by the disciples in inspired language—for this, rather than the rushing noise of wind, is what is meant by 'this sound' in verse 6–because they recognized the indigenous languages and dialects of their native lands. The visitors from lands east of Palestine knew Aramaic, and those from the lands west of Palestine knew Greek, but neither the Aramaic nor Greek was a foreign tongue to the Apostle. The Galilaean accent was easily recognized, as Peter knew to his sorrow on an earlier occasion, but these Galilaeans appeared for the moment to share between them a command of most of the tongues spoke throughout the known world."[11]

As we move from a definition of tongues from Acts 2 we see first, believers being given utterance by the Holy Spirit to speak in other lan-

---

10 A similar occurrence of "astonishment" happens in Acts 4 where the Council is "astonished" (cf. 2:7) at the boldness of Peter and John despite being "uneducated, common men." While the individuals who are astonished are different, the ones who are astonishing them are the same, and Luke uses the same word in 4:13 as he does in 2:7.

11 F. F. Bruce, *The Book of the Acts,* (Grand Rapids: Eerdmans 1997), 59.

guages/tongues (2:4); second, non-believers hearing these believers speak in their own languages which causes astonishment and amazement (2:6, 8, 12); and third, believers declaring to non-believers, in their own languages, the mighty works of God.

God used the speaking in tongues at Pentecost as a means of sharing His mighty works with those who were from *every nation*.[12] The amazement of these unbelievers—that they could hear the mighty works of God in their own tongue by those who didn't speak their own language—led them to question what was happening. Consequently from Acts 2, we can see that the gift of tongues is the speaking in a known language, unknown to the speaker, and is used for the proclamation of the gospel.

The other two times that Luke records instances of tongues in Acts are also incredibly helpful to us, and we read of those events in Acts 10 and Acts 19. However, significantly less information is given about these events as compared with Acts 2, and while there are some similarities between all three events, there are also some striking differences. As we continue, we will have to ask ourselves if the above definition of *tongues* is supported, broadened, or amended.

Tongues in Acts 10

In Acts 10:44–48, we read of the Holy Spirit being poured out on Gentiles who had placed their faith and trust in Jesus Christ. Earlier in Acts 10, we learned that Peter is in Joppa with Simon the tanner, who lived by the sea.

While Peter is praying one afternoon, he is shown a vision from the Lord that commands him to kill and eat animals that Peter understood to be unclean (vv. 11–13). Peter responds to the Lord, "I have never eaten anything that is common or unclean" (v. 14), to which the Lord

---

12 While the mighty works of God (μεγαλεῖα τοῦ θεοῦ) is not defined specifically as the Gospel (εὐαγγέλιον) it is not incorrect to understand these works as containing an explanation of the Gospel. For the mightiest of all of God's works was the resurrection of Jesus, and all the mighty works Jesus Himself did while He was on earth were for the purpose of proclaiming the Gospel and calling sinners to repentance.

replies, "What God has made clean, do not call common" (v. 15). As the story progresses, we learn that God was not only interested in expanding Peter's food options, He was giving him a vivid illustration to tell him that Gentiles would be saved (Acts 10:28)!

Once Peter wakes up from his vision, we are told he is inwardly perplexed and wondering what the vision might mean. At this point, men from Caesarea who had been sent by Cornelius, arrive at Simon's house looking for Peter. Luke tells us, "While Peter was pondering the vision, the Spirit said to him, 'behold, three men are looking for you. Rise and go down and accompany them without hesitation, for I have sent them'" (Acts 10:19–20). Unlike Jonah, who went down to Joppa to run from speaking to the Gentiles about God, Peter is sent by God from Joppa to the Gentiles.

When Peter arrives in Caesarea, he meets Cornelius who has gathered together all his close friends and relatives. Cornelius explains to Peter how, while he was praying, "a man stood before me in bright clothing" and told him to "send therefore to Joppa and ask for Simon who is called Peter" (vv. 30–32). Upon hearing this, Peter opened his mouth and declared the gospel to these people and while he was doing so, "the Holy Spirit fell on all who heard the word" (v. 44).

The Jewish believers who had traveled with Peter were amazed at what took place "because the gift of the Holy Spirit was poured out even on the Gentiles" (v. 45). For, we are told, "they are hearing them speaking in tongues and extolling God" (v. 46). Peter himself, recognizing what had happened, declares that these new Gentile believers should be baptized and recognizes that they "have received the Holy Spirit just as we have" (v. 47).

As noted earlier there are similarities between this passage and Acts 2. However, there are also significant differences. Similarities include: Peter, the preaching of the gospel, baptism upon conversion, speaking in tongues, and the extolling of God. The differences include: a Gentile audience hearing the gospel, and amazement by the Jewish believers that the Holy Spirit was poured on even the Gentiles.

As we try to understand these events, we ought to consider a few other points:

1 The Holy Spirit fell on these Gentile believers; He was not prayed for.
2 Peter did not tell these Gentile believers to confirm their salvation by speaking in tongues.
3 The amazement of the Jewish believers and Peter's own words that they "have received the Holy Spirit just as we have" appears to be the focus of this passage and perhaps the reason why the Holy Spirit fell in this way.

For Peter and the Jewish believers who were with him, God was making it abundantly clear (as if Peter's dream and vision were not enough) that no person should be called clean or unclean, and no distinction should be made between Jewish and Gentile believers (Acts 10:28). Because of God's confirmation there was no potential for them to conclude that there was a qualitative difference in salvation between Jews and Gentiles. These first Gentile believers had spoken in tongues like the Jewish believers who had been in the upper room.

Regarding the exact type of tongues these Gentiles believers spoke, it is simplest for us to understand them as known languages that they did not otherwise know. Supporting this are Peter's and the other Jewish believers' conclusions that the Holy Spirit fell on the Gentiles just like He had them.

Other than Acts 2 there had been no recorded other instances where Peter and these others spoke in tongues, yet the content of their message was the same in Acts 10 as in Acts 2. Luke writes in Acts 10:46 that they were "extolling God"[13] which is nearly identical to what Luke reports in Acts 2:11 that is translated "the mighty works of God."[14]

While the purpose of tongues in Acts 10 appears to be different from the purpose in Acts 2, we are correct in interpreting the speak-

---

13 Gk. μεγαλυνόντων τὸν θεόν.
14 Gk. μεγαλεῖα τοῦ θεοῦ.

91

ing of tongues as the same type of filling and gifting. Bruce writes, "The descent of the Spirit on these Gentiles was outwardly manifested in much the same way as it had been when the original disciples received the Spirit at Pentecost; they spoke with tongues and proclaimed the mighty works of God. Apart from such external manifestations, none of the Jewish Christians present, perhaps not even Peter himself, would have been so ready to accept the fact that the Spirit had really come upon them." [15]

In fact, Peter makes this very point in Acts 11:15–17 when speaking to leaders from the circumcision party who were criticizing him for going to uncircumcised men. Peter defended his actions by stating, "As I began to speak, the Holy Spirit fell on them just as on us at the beginning.[16] And I remembered the word of the Lord, how he said, 'John baptized with water, but you will be baptized with the Holy Spirit.' If then God gave the same gift to them as he gave to us when we believed in the Lord Jesus Christ, who was I that I could stand in God's way?"

Even though the purpose of speaking in tongues appears slightly different in Acts 10, we are repeatedly told that, in the minds of those who were at both events, it was the same gifting of the Holy Spirit. Peter makes it clear he understood the event that took place with the Gentile believers as being *the same gift* as he and the others in the upper room received *in the beginning* (Acts 11:15–17). Specifically, this gifting would have been speaking in *tongues*; however, the miraculous event also indicated that the Holy Spirit had been received as well.

Tongues in Acts 19
In Acts 19, we have the last recorded occurrence of tongues in Luke's historical account of the early church. As we saw in Acts 10, the coming of the Holy Spirit was evidenced by speaking in tongues, confirming that the salvation experienced by these Gentiles was genuine and that God was making no differentiation between ethnicities.

---

15 Bruce, *The Book of Acts,* 229–230.

16 Luke records Peter using the word ὥσπερ to describe the similarities between Acts 2 and Acts 10. BDAG defines this word as "marker of similarity between events and states", and "connecting with what goes before," 1106.

Before concluding that the events of Acts 19 give proof that the Holy Spirit comes with tongues to confirm *all* salvation experiences, we need to be careful and not apply this event further than Luke intends. Luke does not even hint at a widespread experience of tongues by those in Ephesus, and this experience shows up in none of Paul's writings to the Ephesian church.[17] Sam Storms notes in his book *Practicing the Power,* "This is not a paradigmatic event for us today, as no one today lives in this sort of redemptive-historical time warp."

The ESV Study Bible also notes,

> *The Holy Spirit came on them* means they received the new covenant fullness and power of the Holy Spirit, something that happened to Jesus' disciples for the first time on the day of Pentecost. They had not previously known about Jesus' death and resurrection, so their earlier belief (19:2) was one of looking forward to the Messiah to come, a state similar to that of OT believers. *Their speaking in tongues and prophesying* was an outward demonstration and verification of their receiving the Spirit.[18]

The issue in Acts 19 was not an ethnic one between Jews and Gentiles; rather, it was a covenantal one between the disciples of John (Old Covenant) and disciples of Jesus (New Covenant). John Stott writes about these disciples that, "in a word, they were still living in the Old Testament which culminated with John the Baptist. They understood neither that the new age had been ushered in by Jesus, nor that those who believe in him and are baptized into him receive the distinctive blessing of the new age, the indwelling Spirit."[19]

Unlike Acts 10, we have no reaction from Paul that indicates a purpose for these tongues, or even surprise that they happened for that matter. Unlike Acts 2, the number of individuals speaking in tongues

---

17 Sam Storms, *Practicing the Power,* (Grand Rapids: Zondervan, 2017), 42.

18 John B. Polhill. *ESV Study Bible.* N.19:6. p. 2125.

19 John Stott, *The Spirit the Church and the World: The Message of Acts* (Downers Grove, InterVarsity Press, 1990), 304

was considerably fewer. In Acts 2, there were about 120 persons who spoke in tongues. Here there are only about 12 men.

Acts 19 is best understood similarly to how we have understood Acts 10. It was a unique event that occurred during a highly transitory period for the church. Acts 10 speaks to an ethnic transition, and Acts 19 speaks to a covenantal transition.[20] Neither Acts 10 nor Acts 19 defines the speaking in tongues differently than how Luke does in Acts 2. Furthermore, Acts 10 and 11 specifically record that the speaking in tongues happened for the Gentiles the *same* way it did for the Jews.

In summary, within the book of Acts, Luke defines tongues as the speaking in a known language, unknown to the speaker, that is used for the proclamation of the gospel. Although a salvation confirming aspect of *tongues* is present in Acts 10 and 19, there is no specific command that *all* believers must speak in tongues, nor any further indication that more believers spoke in tongues than the ones specifically recorded as doing so.

---

20 It is also significant to note that the Ethiopian eunuch is not recorded to have spoken in tongues upon his conversion even though he was a Gentile who placed his faith in Jesus Christ. It appears then that Peter specifically was to see the Holy Spirit coming in the same way to the Gentiles as the Spirit did to the Jews.

12

TONGUES IN
1 CORINTHIANS 12–14

As we now begin to consider specifically what Paul wrote to the Corinthians regarding the spiritual gift of tongues, we would do well to pause and observe a few important facts:

1. In Acts, Luke never records that the church in Corinth spoke in tongues despite Paul being with them for 18 months.[1]

2. Paul never cites speaking in tongues as confirming evidence for the Corinthians' salvation experience.

3. Paul never cites speaking in tongues as confirmation that the Holy Spirit lives in them.

In 1 Corinthians, Paul's use of *tongues* (γλωσσα) occurs most frequently in chapter 14, and one of the particular interpretive challenges we face in 1 Corinthians 14 is that Paul specifically references all three categories of meaning that *tongues* may have.[2] In fact, if 1 Corinthians 14 did not exist, or if Paul had not written about ecstatic utterances or unintelligible speech, the conversation surrounding *tongues* would be a much simpler one. Nevertheless, God has spoken, and it is in our best interest to draw near and listen.

---

1 This observation is not to insinuate that they didn't speak in tongues, it is however, to observe the limited record of tongues experiences and note the absence of any city-wide tongues experience.

2 See chapter 10.

TO EACH IS GIVEN

Interpretive Challenges

Throughout chapter 14 interpretive challenges abound, and as we seek to understand what the spiritual gifts of *tongues* is, we will be well served by understanding that Paul aims to draw a distinction between the singular and plural uses of *tongue(s)*. Paul's use of both the singular and plural forms of *tongue(s)*; occur eight and seven times respectively.[3]

For example, if *a tongue* (singular) and *tongues* (plural) are one and the same gift that Paul writes about in chapter 12, then we must reconcile how there is consistent emphasis on *tongues* being a known language, that can be translated, in both Acts and even 1 Corinthians 14, and *a tongue* being described as mysterious utterances and intelligible speech. However, if *a tongue* and *tongues* are not the same gift then, in obedience to Paul's command in chapter 14 verse 1 to *earnestly desire the spiritual gifts*, there should be no pursuit of *a tongue* because it is fruitless, unintelligible speech.

Another interpretive challenge lies with the interpretation that *tongue(s)* can be used as a personal prayer language. Advocating this position, Sam Storms writes, "First of all, speaking in tongues is a form of prayer. 1 Corinthians 14:2 Paul says that speaking in tongues is speaking 'to God' (see also vs. 28). Again, in verses 14–15 he explicitly refers to 'praying' in tongues or 'praying' with (by) his spirit."[4] However, to adopt this position, we must reconcile how this personal prayer language fits with Paul's overall assertion that spiritual gifts build up the entire church and are not primarily for the individual.

This interpretation of *personal prayer language* is foreign to the entire context of 1 Corinthians 12–14, where Paul writes about the interdependency of the body and states that spiritual gifts have been given for the building up of the body, not just one member! Storms'

---

3 See table 1.

4 Wayne Grudem, Richard Gaffin, Robert Saucy, Sam Storms, and Douglas Oss, *Are Miraculous Gifts for Today? 4 Views* (Grand Rapids: Zondervan, 1996), 215.

assertion is problematic in that a personal prayer language only benefits the one speaking and not the entire body.

At the heart of the debate regarding tongues, there appear to be three questions we must answer:

1. Does Paul list two types of tongues? Or, to ask it another way, are there tongues for public worship and a tongue for private worship?

2. If there are two types of tongues, are they the same in their usefulness?

3. Is the spiritual gift of tongues for use in corporate worship? And if so, how?

Looking at 1 Corinthians 14 in greater detail will be helpful to see exactly what Paul writes regarding *tongue(s)*. What follows is each verse where *tongue(s)* occurs in 1 Corinthians 14.[5]

1 Corinthians 14:2

"For one who speaks in a *tongue* speaks not to men but to God; for no one understands him, but he utters mysteries in the Spirit."

1 Corinthians 14:4

"The one who speaks in a *tongue* builds up himself, but the one who prophesies builds up the church."

1 Corinthians 14:5

"Now I want you all to speak in *tongues,* but even more to prophesy. The one who prophesies is greater than the one who speaks in *tongues*, unless someone interprets, so that the church may be built up."

1 Corinthians 14:6

"Now, brothers, if I come to you speaking in *tongues*, how will I benefit you unless I bring you some revelation or knowledge or prophecy or teaching?"

---

5 Emphasis mine.

To Each Is Given

1 Corinthians 14:9
"So with yourselves, if with your *tongue* you utter speech that is not intelligible, how will anyone know what is said? For you will be speaking into the air."

1 Corinthians 14:13
"Therefore, one who speaks in a *tongue* should pray that he may interpret."

1 Corinthians 14:14
"For if I pray in a *tongue*, my spirit prays but my mind is unfruitful."

1 Corinthians 14:18
"I thank God that I speak in *tongues* more than all of you."

1 Corinthians 14:19
"Nevertheless, in church I would rather speak five words with my mind in order to instruct others, than ten thousand words in a *tongue*."

1 Corinthians 14:21
"In the Law it is written, 'By people of strange *tongues* and by the lips of foreigners will I speak to this people, and even then they will not listen to me, says the Lord.'"

1 Corinthians 14:22
"Thus *tongues* are a sign not for believers but for unbelievers, while prophecy is a sign not for unbelievers but for believers."

1 Corinthians 14:23
"If, therefore, the whole church comes together and all speak in *tongues*, and outsiders or unbelievers enter, will they not say that you are out of your minds?"

1 Corinthians 14:26
"What then, brothers? When you come together, each one has a hymn, a lesson, a revelation, a *tongue*, or an interpretation. Let all things be done for building up."

1 Corinthians 14:27
"If any speak in a *tongue,* let there be only two or at most three, and each in turn, and let someone interpret."

1 Corinthians 14:39

"So, my brothers, earnestly desire to prophesy, and do not forbid speaking in *tongues*."

Question 1:

Does Paul list two types of tongues? Or, to ask it another way, are there tongues for public worship and a tongue for private worship?

Throughout chapter 14, the Apostle Paul appears to draw a distinction between two types of tongue experiences. One builds up the individual, while the other builds up the church. Regarding these two, Paul uses the singular form *tongue* to reference the individual experience and the plural form of *tongues* to reference what builds up the church.[6] John MacArthur helpfully notes, "It is an interpretive key to this chapter to note that in verses 2 and 4 *tongue* is singular (cf. verses 13,14,19, [26], 27), whereas in verse 5 Paul uses the plural *tongues* (cf. verses 6, 18, 22, 23, 29). Apparently, the apostle used the singular form to indicate the counterfeited gift and the plural to indicate the true."[7]

Using the singular form of *tongue,* Paul writes in 1 Corinthians 14:2 "for one who speaks in a tongue speaks not to me but to God; for no one understands him, but he utters mysteries in the Spirit." Later in verse 14:4 we read, "the one who speaks in a tongue builds up himself." However, using the plural in verse 14:5 Paul states that interpreted tongues build up the church.

Regarding the claim that *tongues* can be for private worship/prayer several things stand out as significant. First, Paul uses the singular to note this worship/prayer language. Secondly, the only person being built up is the individual speaking. Thirdly, while Paul has not spoken yet about the usefulness of this experience, he does clearly indicate

---

6 Similarly, we see Paul's use of the singular and plural for *power/miracles* throughout 1 Corinthians to communicate two different ideas. The singular is used in reference to our triune God and his power in working salvation through the Gospel (1:18, 1:24, 2:4, 2:5, 4:20, 5:4, 6:14, 15:24, 15:43) The plural is used in references to the Holy Spirit and the gifts of miracles (1 Cor. 12:10, 28, 29). There is also one use of *power* (sing.) used in reference to sin (1 Cor. 15:56).

7 MacArthur, *1 Corinthians*, 373. Emphasis his.

that *a tongue* used for private worship/prayer does not accomplish the same purposes as spiritual gifts do, namely building up the body.

The idea of a private worship/prayer language for the benefit of just one individual is foreign to Paul's metaphor of a body being interdependent with itself. Paul asserts that the Holy Spirit has gifted every individual within the church with a manifestation that is for the common good (1 Cor. 12:7) or building up of the church (1 Cor. 14:12).

Taking all of this into consideration, we may conclude that the private worship/prayer language of *a tongue* (singular) is different from the public spiritual gift of *tongues* (plural). Furthermore, if what is concluded above is interpretively sound, then we must ask a follow-up question that has tremendous significance. Why would we want any gift that only benefits ourselves?[8] The context is straightforward, *a tongue* as a worship/prayer language does not benefit the church and does not fit with the definition and purpose of spiritual gifts that Paul gives.

If it is true that the singular *tongue* refers to mysterious utterances and the plural *tongues* refers to known languages that are unknown by the speaker, then inserting these definitions into the text should contextually fit what Paul has written and make sense.

Here again, is the list of verses in 1 Corinthians 14 where Paul uses *tongue(s)*. The singular and plural occurrences have been replaced with *mysterious utterances* and *known languages* respectively.

1 Corinthians 14:2

"For one who speaks in a *mysterious utterance* speaks not to men but to God; for no one understands him, but he utters mysteries in the Spirit."

---

8 Contra Storms who seeks to point out that an individual benefiting from the use of their spiritual gift is not a bad thing. He writes, "If I am edified by my gift in such a way that I become more mature, sensitive, understanding, zealous, and holy, and thus better equipped to minister to others, why should anyone complain? The fact that the ultimate purpose of gifts is the common good does not preclude other, secondary effects of each manifestation" (*Miraculous Gifts: 4 Views*, 216). What Storms does not take into account in his statement is that Paul is not indicating that a secondary effect of *a tongue* is individual edification, he is indicating the primary effect is individual edification. There remains a distinct difference between spiritual gifts and "a tongue." Paul is not writing about the byproduct of spiritual gifts, which indeed do all the things Storm lists.

1 Corinthians 14:4
"The one who speaks in a *mysterious utterance* builds up himself, but the one who prophesies builds up the church."

1 Corinthians 14:5
"Now I want you all to speak in *known languages*, but even more to prophesy. The one who prophesies is greater than the one who speaks in *known languages*, unless someone interprets, so that the church may be built up."

1 Corinthians 14:6
"Now, brothers, if I come to you speaking in *known languages*, how will I benefit you unless I bring you some revelation or knowledge or prophecy or teaching?"

1 Corinthians 14:9
"So with yourselves, if with your *mysterious utterance* you utter speech that is not intelligible, how will anyone know what is said? For you will be speaking into the air."

1 Corinthians 14:13
"Therefore, one who speaks in a *mysterious utterance* should pray that he may interpret."

1 Corinthians 14:14
"For if I pray in a *mysterious utterance*, my spirit prays but my mind is unfruitful."

1 Corinthians 14:18
"I thank God that I speak in *known languages*, more than all of you."

1 Corinthians 14:19
"Nevertheless, in church I would rather speak five words with my mind in order to instruct others, than ten thousand words in a *mysterious utterance*."

1 Corinthians 14:21
"In the Law it is written, "By people of strange *known languages*, and by the lips of foreigners will I speak to this people, and even then, they will not listen to me, says the Lord.""

TO EACH IS GIVEN

1 Corinthians 14:22
"Thus *known languages* are a sign not for believers but for unbelievers, while prophecy is a sign not for unbelievers but for believers."

1 Corinthians 14:23
"If, therefore, the whole church comes together and all speak in *known languages*, and outsiders or unbelievers enter, will they not say that you are out of your minds?"

1 Corinthians 14:26
"What then, brothers? When you come together, each one has a hymn, a lesson, a revelation, a *mysterious utterance*, or an interpretation. Let all things be done for building up."[9]

1 Corinthians 14:27
"If any speak in a *known language*, let there be only two or at most three, and each in turn, and let someone interpret."[10]

1 Corinthians 14:39
"So, my brothers, earnestly desire to prophesy, and do not forbid speaking in *known languages*."

Rather than seeing 1 Corinthians 14:2 as permission for *a tongue* to be used as worship/prayer language, we must see that Paul is leading the Corinthians to ask themselves why they would even want such a gift if it does not benefit the body. This point becomes all the more relevant when considered against the backdrop of the Corinthian church, which appears to have had people speaking in these mysterious utterances and unintelligible sounds. Paul was not giving com-

---

9 Admittedly, the interpretation I am proposing sees v. 26 as first a statement of correction about Corinthian behavior, and secondly as a command for Corinthian behavior. Therein, Paul is first asking a rhetorical question about the numerous and disorderly things taking place in the worship service and then instructs the Corinthians to focus on building up others. For our purposes it is important to remember that the one who utters mysteries in a tongue does not build up the church (cf. 14:1-5).

10 *Tongue* is singular here, not plural and is used this way for grammatical reasons. So MacArthur explains, "the only exception is in v. 27, where the singular is used to refer to a single man speaking a single genuine language." *1 Corinthians,* 373.

mendation for their use of a private worship/prayer language; he was providing correction.

Question 2:

If there are two types of tongue(s), are they the same in their usefulness?

To answer this question and help the Corinthians apply his teaching, Paul inserts a hypothetical scenario that begins in 1 Corinthians 14:6 regarding the purpose of the spiritual gift of *tongues*. He writes, "Now, brothers, if I come to you speaking in tongues, how will I benefit you unless I bring you some revelation or knowledge or prophecy or teaching?"

Paul sees tongues as useful in communicating information, not as simply gibberish, and he is not interested in unintelligible speech that does not benefit, or build up the church! This is why directly after he writes that interpreted tongues build up the church (v. 5) he continues this thought and writes about revelation, knowledge, prophecy, or teaching.[11]

In verses 7–8, Paul illustrates his point by presenting two analogies to help them, and us, understand what he is saying. The first is of a musical instrument, which is intended to play distinct notes at the right time within a piece of music, such as the flute or harp. Musicians do not merely play random notes whenever they feel like it, and if they did, there would be no added benefit to the overall piece of music.

Perhaps it is helpful for us to think about Paul's illustration in the context of an elementary school student bringing home their new instrument from band class. In this experience many parents and siblings have firsthand knowledge of Paul's point. The indistinct notes played by a first-time musician can be painful to listen to and make little musical contribution, if any. These novice musicians are contrasted with professionals who skillfully play their instrument in the

---

11 This also fits what we saw in Acts 2 and Acts 10 in that the tongues communicate information—"the mighty works of God."

right way. The distinct and recognizable notes played by the skilled player are beautiful, fitting, timely, and purposeful. As a result, the entire band or orchestra benefits from individual contribution.

In verse 8, Paul continues and provides a second analogy about a bugle giving sound to soldiers. Unlike in today's world, the call to battle was not given through walkie-talkies or other high tech means of communication. Soldiers mobilized and prepared for battle upon hearing a bugle play the predetermined, distinct sound for which they had been instructed to listen.

Think about how unorganized an army would be if soldiers did not have a predetermined alert system. Some soldiers might move before the right time; others might not move at all. The enemy would have a decisive advantage amid the chaos! Highly trained and prepared militaries use distinct signals to communicate and avoid disaster. Proper communication within the ranks of an army during a battle may be the difference between victory and defeat, life and death.

Paul's point is that for tongues to build up and be beneficial for the church they must be distinct, recognizable, and able to be interpreted, or else there is no benefit. Here, once again, a clear contrast is drawn between mysterious, unintelligible, speech, and known languages that can be translated and understood.

Moving from these two illustrations, Paul now specifically reemphasizes what he is saying. In verse 9, he writes, "So with yourselves, if with your tongue you utter speech that is not intelligible, how will anyone know what is said? For you will be speaking into the air." [12] Once again, we see Paul make his point that speaking is for the purpose of communicating. Unintelligible, or mysterious, utterances do not benefit because no one knows what is being said.

Providing one final illustration in verses 10–11, Paul aims to further drive his point home. He now writes about someone interacting with another who speaks a different language.

In July of 2016, my wife and I boarded a plane and flew to China to adopt our son Toban. With tremendous excitement and nervousness,

---

12 The only reference in 1 Corinthians to the bodily organ.

we flew for over 13 hours and landed in Beijing. We were now in a different country, and we didn't know the language!

While in the airport, our inability to speak Chinese was mitigated by the numerous signs printed in English and the many airport employees who were able to direct us with words we could understand. Perhaps most importantly, the Starbucks logo has always looked the same no matter where in the world I am!

However, after we left the airport and began to travel into the city center of Beijing, we were fully confronted with the reality that we don't speak or read Chinese! Despite having a travel guide who doubled as our translator, we were keenly aware that we were foreigners.

On our second day in Beijing, we felt brave enough to venture out on our own to find some dinner. I remember repeating to myself over and over again the name of the shopping mall we were looking for so that if we got lost, I could utter a few words in Chinese that would help a local resident guide us ... and it happened! We had to stop and ask a Chinese soldier how to find the mall.

The soldier was standing guard on the sidewalk with a fully automatic rifle, and I approached him with a desperate "help us please" look. Shrugging my shoulders, I uttered the name of the mall, and probably looked like a lost puppy dog! He pointed down the road, and we understood that he was telling us to keep walking. Thankfully we were just a few blocks away.

Paul's point is this: if known languages remain uninterpreted, or not understood, there is no benefit to those who are trying to communicate! Language is intended to communicate information. When we do not know the language, significant challenges abound.

I had to learn the name of the Chinese mall so that I could say it in the language of the Chinese soldier who, more than likely, would not have understood my English. Therefore, if real languages remain uninterpreted and not understood they do not benefit, how much less beneficial are unintelligible tongues!

Speaking *mysteries in the spirit* (1 Cor. 14:2) does not build up the church and is consequently not beneficial for the church. Rather than striving for these mysterious utterances, which no one can understand, the Corinthians are to strive to excel in building up one another (1 Cor. 14:12).[13]

Through verse 12 of 1 Corinthians 14, Paul has specifically written about building up the body five different times![14] Throughout chapter 14 Paul uses either the verb or noun form of *building up* seven times![15] His consistent and repeated emphasis on the church being built up must be recognized. His concern is for the building up of the church, and this fits the purpose of what a spiritual gift is from 1 Corinthians 12:7. In 1 Corinthians 12:7, we are told that "each is given the manifestation of the Spirit for the common good."

Therefore, if a tongue does not build up the church, it is not for the *common good*, and should not be *earnestly desired*. In obedience to Paul's command in verse 1, we should not be desiring the mysterious utterances that Paul speaks of, which do not build up the church because it is not a spiritual gift (vv. 14:2, 9).

Shifting from illustrations and analogies, Paul now begins in verse 13 to apply what he has just said. He begins with a command for the individual who may speak "mysteries in the spirit" (v. 14:2) or things that are not "intelligible" (v. 14:9) and commands them to "pray that he may interpret." Once again, the emphasis is on the communication of information as a means to build up the church, not gibberish that is "speaking into the air."

An interesting component to Paul's command in verse 13 is his instruction later in chapter 14 about the public speaking of tongues and how someone other than the individual speaking in tongues should interpret what is said.[16] Because of this we must be cautious in seeing verse 13 as a green light for the use of unintelligible speech as long as the one speaking can provide an interpretation, for this still does not

---

13 A point Paul first introduces in 1 Cor. 3:10–15.

14 14:3, 4(x2), 5, 12.

15 14:3, 4(x2), 5, 12, 17, 26.

16 In these later instructions, he will continue to emphasize his point that unintelligent speech is not to be pursued.

fit the definition of tongues or the use of spiritual gifts! To pray with a specific request is to pray with specific words. It is not to pray with unintelligible words. Paul is telling them to focus their prayers on intelligible words because intelligible words are beneficial.

To best understand what Paul is saying in verses 14–19, it is best to take a step back and remind ourselves of what he has said up to this point. The Corinthian church has written to him asking about certain spiritual people who are trying to draw attention to themselves and demeaning those who do not appear to be as spiritual. To answer these questions, Paul tells them first that only those who claim Jesus is Lord are truly spiritual, and second, among those who claim Jesus is Lord, there is no hierarchy of spiritual gifts.

Taking this context, and Paul's treatment of unintelligible utterances in 14:1–12, a clearer picture of this local church begins to emerge. Not only were there spiritual people in this congregation saying Jesus is accursed, but also some who loved Jesus erred by believing that they were more spiritual than others because they were able to speak in a tongue. They saw their *gift* as more supernatural than the gift of discernment or faith and consequently were putting themselves forward as those who were better or more spiritual. Yet, there is no special class of individuals who have a greater indwelling of the Holy Spirit than any other persons, and the claims of some that they are more spiritual because they speak in mysterious utterances must be rejected.

However, Paul is unwilling to denounce all tongues outright. He knows that God has used tongues for His glory in the past and that the Holy Spirit does still apportion and empower the speaking and interpreting of tongues through individuals who have been given that gift. Thus, in chapter 14, Paul writes about a distinction between mysterious utterances and languages that can be translated and understood, and he makes the point that one is to be kept because it is profitable and builds up, while the other does not.

As Paul further applies his instructions in verses 13–19, he overstates his point by providing a hypothetical example regarding the tension between intelligent words and unintelligible words. Concluding his own arguments in verse 19, he writes, "Nevertheless, in church I would rather speak five words with my mind in order to instruct others, than ten thousand words in a tongue," and with this summary Paul's distinction between unintelligible speech and intelligible words that benefit gains further clarity.

In verse 14, Paul shares a hypothetical struggle that he resolves for his readers in verse 15. He writes, "For if I pray in a tongue, my spirit prays but my mind is unfruitful. What am I to do? I will pray with my spirit, but I will pray with my mind also; I will sing praise with my spirit, but I will sing with my mind also." Paul's point is that he wants praying and singing that is intelligible and fruitful. Consequently, in this hypothetical situation, Paul will no longer "pray in a tongue" for to do so would be unfruitful for his mind, which is exactly what he does not want!

For the Corinthians, and the church today, this must not be missed. The foundation of Christianity is built upon the Apostles and Prophets, and Jesus Christ is the cornerstone (Eph. 2:20). These Apostles, Prophets, and Jesus Christ himself came speaking words! Words that could be understood! Words that accorded with known languages. Words that imparted, and still impart, spiritual life!

The church in Corinth, and our churches today, should only be focused on speech that is intelligible and accords with sound doctrine.[17] This is what Paul told Timothy to pass on to faithful men (2 Tim. 2:2) and what he told Titus to pass on to the church in Crete (Titus 2:1); and this is exactly what Paul himself did whenever he planted a church or wrote a letter to a local church. It may be novel or even

---

17 Contra *The Full Life Study Bible* which asserts that "speaking in tongues involves the human spirit and the Spirit of God intermingling so that the believer communicates directly to God (i.e. prayer, praise, blessing or thanksgiving), giving expression or utterance at the level of one's spirit rather than the mind (1 Cor. 14:2, 14) and praying for oneself or others under the direct influence of the Holy Spirit apart from the activity of the mind." Donald C. Stamps, *The Full Life Study Bible— New Testament* (Grand Rapids: Zondervan, 1990), 351. This statement infers that prayer, not in a tongue, does not communicate directly to God. This then begs to the question, who does prayer communicate to?

seem spiritual to speak in mysterious utterances that no one can understand; however, it is not helpful! Paul continues to unfold these truths in verses 16–18.

In verse 16, Paul gives another example of how a tongue is unfruitful and does not build up others. He writes about a person speaking in mysterious utterances being convinced that they are giving thanks to God for something. Yet, those around him are unable to participate in this expression of praise because they don't understand what is being said. Consequently, even though someone may be fully convinced that their unintelligible speech is giving thanks to God, it still is unfruitful because others in the body are not built up.

Throughout chapters 12–14, Paul consistently emphasizes believers being together, and verses 16–17 repeat this emphasis.[18] Despite the claims that the gift of tongues can be a private prayer language, Paul never once references a tongue as a private worship/prayer language spoken in the privacy of one's home.

The following verses, 18–19, also make sense if we allow for tongues to be Paul's way of referring to known languages unknown to the speaker, in contrast to unintelligible words spoken in a tongue. Paul is thankful that he speaks in known languages unknown to him (*tongues*) more than all of those in Corinth.

Tongues are real, and the Holy Spirit does apportion and empower the gift of tongues. Known languages build up the church, mysterious utterances do not. Here Paul is upholding and affirming this spiritual gift as it relates to the true purpose of tongues.

In verse 19, Paul caps off his hypothetical argument by making a statement of hyperbole and again places emphasis on the value of language that instructs and can be understood. Rather than 10,000 words that no one can understand, he wants five words that can be understood!

---

18 The same emphasis is present in 1 Cor. 14:2 where Paul writes, "for no one understands him …" The person speaking in *a tongue* is always in the presence of others. Paul provides no analogy, illustration, or situation where a person is alone.

To Each Is Given

By the time we arrive at 1 Corinthians 14:20–25, we have learned the following:

1. Spiritual gifts are to be earnestly desired (14:1, 12).

2. Spiritual gifts build up the church and are for the common good (12:7; 14:3, 4b, 5, 12, 26).

3. Mysterious utterances and unintelligible speech do not build up the church and therefore are not spiritual gifts (14:4, 9).

4. Believers are commanded to strive to excel in building up the church (14:12).

5. Paul wants the church in Corinth filled with intelligible words that can be understood and provide instruction (14:5–6, 19).

The modern-day fascination with unintelligible speech is without biblical support and should not be pursued. Even as a private worship/prayer language, unintelligible speech does not benefit the body and should not be pursued. What should be pursued is speech that is fruitful for one's mind (v. 14), builds up the body (v. 17), and instructs (v. 19).

Question 3:

Is the spiritual gift of tongues for use in corporate worship? And if so, how?

The spiritual gift of tongues is still for the church today. It will cease in the new heavens and new earth when believers are with Christ forevermore; seeing "face to face" and "knowing fully" (1 Cor. 13:12). Ciampa and Rosner write about prophecy, tongues, and knowledge, and when they will come to an end, stating,

> It should be understood that these three gifts are chosen merely as examples so that what is said about them is understood to apply to the other spiritual gifts as well. There is nothing about the middle voice to suggest that tongues would stop or come to an end at any point time other than that which is clarified in the following verses—at the final consummation.[19]

19 Ciampa and Rosner, *The First Letter to the Corinthians*, 655.

To this Fee adds,

> Thus Paul's point with all of this is now made. He began (v.
> 8) by arguing that love, in contrast to the *charismata*, never
> comes to an end. Preciously because the gifts have an end
> point, which love does not, they are of a different order ...
> they will pass away (v. 8); they are "in part" (v. 9); they be-
> long to this present existence only (vv. 10–12) ... As good
> as the Spirit's giftings are, they are nonetheless only for the
> present; sacrificial love, which the Corinthians currently
> lack, is the "more excellent way" in part because it belongs
> to eternity as well as to the present.[20]

Regarding the *perfect* of 1 Cor. 13:10 John MacArthur writes, "Paul
is saying that spiritual gifts are only for a time, but that love will last
for all eternity. The point is simple, not obscure. The eternal state
allows for the form of *the perfect* and allows for the continuation of
knowledge and prophecy during the church age, the Tribulation, and
the Kingdom."[21]

Until the new heavens and new earth, we are commanded to love
first and foremost and earnestly desire spiritual gifts (1 Cor. 14:2);
continuing to be "eager for manifestations of the Spirit" (1 Cor.
14:12). Specifically, regarding tongues, we are "not to forbid speaking in tongues" (1 Cor. 14:39).

In Acts 2, we saw that tongues are speaking in a known language,
unknown to the speaker, and used for the proclamation of the gospel
in a situation where a nonbeliever would otherwise not be able to understand what is said. As we have observed throughout 1 Corinthians
14, thus far, the spiritual gift of tongues is the speaking of a known
language that is unknown to the speaker. Paul's explanation of the gift
of tongues in 1 Corinthians 14 fits exactly with what Luke records in
Acts 2.

---

20 Fee. *The First Epistle to the Corinthians*, 719.

21 MacArthur, *1 Corinthians.*, 365–366. Notably, MacArthur does believe that
tongues have ceased with the end of the apostolic age (p. 359). Emphasis his.

TO EACH IS GIVEN

Throughout verses 1–19, the Apostle Paul is primarily dealing with unintelligent utterances that carry no meaning and do not benefit the body of Christ in any way. Beginning in verse 20, he shifts his attention to known languages, remaining uninterpreted, being spoken within a corporate worship gathering.

The key to interpreting verses 20–25 is understanding what Paul intends to communicate through his quotation of Isaiah. To do this, we need to understand what God had originally communicated to and through Isaiah. Quoting Isaiah 28:11–12, Paul writes, "By people of strange tongues and by the lips of foreigners will I speak to this people, and even then, they will not listen to me, says the Lord."

Regarding Isaiah 28:1–29 in its original context Ciampa and Rosner write, "Isaiah 28:11–12 indicates that God would speak to his people in judgement through a strange language because they did not listen to him earlier when he spoke in clear and simple terms."[22]

> To this, G.K. Beale and D.A. Carson add, "Isaiah 28:1–29 consists of an oracle against the political and religious leadership of God's people (Samaria and Jerusalem). They had rejected God's counsel to rest and trust in him as being naïve and had gone ahead in a policy marked by a drunken madness and formed other alliances. The leadership (rulers, priests, and prophets) refused to listen when God clearly and plainly explained to them what it meant to rest in him and to give rest to the weary, so now God's voice of judgement will be heard in the barbarian language of the Assyrian invaders."[23]

God was judging Israel for her disobedience and unbelief and was using the Assyrian army to do so. As we begin to understand what God has spoken to the prophet Isaiah regarding his people, Paul's use of this passage and its application becomes clear. Uninterpreted languages are a sign of judgment, not of blessing. Returning to a point

---

22 Ciampa and Rosner, *The First Letter to the Corinthians*, 700.

23 G.K. Beale, and D.A. Carson, *Commentary on the New Testament Use of the Old Testament* (Grand Rapids: Baker Academic, 2007), 740.

made earlier regarding unintelligent utterances may help us understand the significance of what Paul says here.

The gospel message came in words. The Word became flesh and made His dwelling among us (John 1:14). Jesus came speaking words as Mark records for us, "Jesus came into Galilee, proclaiming the gospel of God ... " (Mark 1:14). This gospel was then entrusted to the Apostles who declared this good news to others, who in turn declare it to others. To believe that God now communicates to His people through languages they cannot understand, or that unbelievers will come into a chaotic worship service and be convicted through words they cannot understand, is at best misguided.

Regarding these unbelievers, Paul writes in 1 Corinthians 14:23 that these unbelievers who come in will conclude that "you are out of your mind." Therefore, strange tongues (known languages that remain uninterpreted) are both a sign of God's judgment and the exact opposite of a compelling gospel witness.

Furthermore, to state his point more clearly, he contrasts tongues once again with prophecy and speaks to the greater value of prophecy because unbelievers will be convicted by the "secrets of their hearts being disclosed" (1 Cor. 14:24–25). God's blessing is experienced in the clear understanding of His word and the gospel message! Sadly, what many charismatics today seek as God's blessing is actually a sign of His judgment.

Paul specifically confirms this understanding in verse 22, writing, "Thus tongues are a sign not for believers but for unbelievers." Carson writes, "it appears, then, that when God speaks through strange tongues and the lips of foreigners, at least here it is, a sign of his judgment upon them."[24] Wayne Grudem adds, "Paul understands very well that when God speaks to people in a language they cannot understand, it is a form of punishment for unbelief. Incomprehensible speech will not guide but confuse and lead to destruction. And it is one of the last in a series of divine rebukes, none of which have produced the desired repentance and obedience."[25]

---

24 Carson, *Showing the Spirit*, 114.

25 Grudem, *The Gift of Prophecy*, 146.

Those today who are chasing and receiving tongues in their worship services are receiving divine judgment from God and are being identified by God as unbelievers, even though they may be fully convinced they are following the Lord. Gordon Fee paraphrases Paul's words in this passage when he writes, "[uninterpreted tongues] are not, as you make them, divine evidence of being *pneumatikos*, nor of the presence of God in your assembly. To the contrary, in the public gathering uninterpreted tongues, function as a sign for unbelievers.... [that of] divine disapproval."[26]

In this regard, they may be like those in Matthew 7:21–23,

> Not everyone who says to me, 'Lord, Lord,' will enter the kingdom of heaven, but the one who does the will of my Father who is in heaven. On that day many will say to me, 'Lord, Lord, did we not prophesy in your name, and cast out demons in your name, and do many mighty works in your name?' And then will I declare to them, 'I never knew you; depart from me, you workers of lawlessness.'

This is exactly what the Lord did with unbelieving Israel as they steadfastly refused to listen to what He was clearly communicating to them through the prophets. As a result of their disobedience and unbelief, the Lord brought in the Assyrians to conquer them. Bruce writes, "When Isaiah warned his fellow-citizens of the folly of their ways, they mocked him for using baby-talk...accordingly he assured them that, since they would not listen to Yahweh's lesson when it was communicated in elementary Hebrew, they would learn it from the foreign speech of Assyrian invaders."[27]

God speaks to His people in words that can be understood and words that provide instruction to them. Beale and Carson continue, "... just as the experience in Isa. 28:11–12 did not result in the conversion of the hearers but instead expressed alienation between God and his people, so also Paul indicated that the use of tongues in

---

26 Fee, *The First Epistle to the Corinthians*, 756.
27 Bruce, *I & II Corinthians*, 132.

church will result not in the conversion of unbelievers but rather in their further alienation."[28]

Garland also notes, "When God speaks intelligibly, it is to reveal. When God speaks unintelligibly, it is to judge. In the Corinthian context, speaking in "other tongues" will fail to convey any meaningful message or bring repentance, just as it failed to do in Isaiah's day. The citation from Isaiah makes clear that tongues are not a saving sign but a sign of retribution. They do not stimulate to believe but instead seal unbelief."[29]

The presence of uninterpreted tongues within a worship service serves as a sign of judgment to a disobedient and unbelieving people, indicating that they are not following the Lord.

Before we go any further, a point of explanation needs to be made. No person can conclusively determine the salvation of another. We can see the fruit of salvation, and we can hear the testimony of individuals who have placed their faith in Christ, but we can only reasonably determine if they are saved. We cannot conclusively determine if they are saved.

Therefore, the above conclusion is not intended to be a wholesale, wide-sweeping condemnation of every single attendee within charismatic or Pentecostal churches.[30] My goal is to faithfully interpret and apply God's Word, and I believe God has given great clarity, through Paul's use of Isaiah 28, regarding the sign of uninterpreted known languages within churches.

If you are in such a church, I plead with you to not read this conclusion as one of arrogant damnation but rather as one of humble pleading. Do not be like unbelieving Israel, who so steadfastly refused to listen to God's clear instructions that He sent foreign languages as a

---

28 Fee, *The First Epistle to the Corinthians*, 742.

29 Garland, *1 Corinthians*, 648.

30 I fully realize my words are harsh and potentially unsettling. However, I do not write them to be unkind. I write them to warn, and do so, I believe, with the authority of the Scriptures. If my conclusions are shown to be in error, I will certainly reconsider them. Nevertheless, regardless of the rightness of my conclusions I pray that my tone is gracious and loving.

form of judgment. And if you find yourself in such judgment, recognize that even in judgment God is still gracious, rich in mercy, slow to anger, and abounding in steadfast love.[31]

Lastly, tongues also serve as a sign to unbelievers who do not know they are unbelievers, or those who have not yet heard the gospel. In this sense, tongues would be a positive sign to them of God's desire to communicate to them, in their own language, by those who may not speak their own language. This is why Paul does not forbid the speaking of tongues (v. 39) and accords with how we see tongues functioning in Acts 2.

The picture then of these two uses is as follows. Those claiming to be gathered in the name of the Lord Jesus receiving tongues that remain uninterpreted is a sign of judgment for they are unable to understand what God is saying to them. Those who do not know the Lord Jesus and who may hear the gospel in their own tongues receive a positive sign from God just as those gathered in Acts 2 did.

How exactly, then, are the spiritual gifts of tongues used, and how do we obey the command in 1 Corinthians 14:39 and not forbid the speaking in tongues? Answers to these questions lie in the next set of verses and in the definition of tongues that we have been working with.

Rather than everyone speaking in known languages that are unknown to them, the two or three who have a tongue are permitted to speak—each in turn and with interpretation.[32] By introducing these two points of criteria that must be met, we learn again that Paul is not willing to simply dismiss the spiritual gift of tongues.

In Acts 2, known languages that were unknown to the speaker were spoken and used by the Holy Spirit to communicate with those in Jerusalem who would not otherwise have heard the mighty works of God proclaimed. In Corinth, the Holy Spirit may have empowered

---

31 Exodus 34:6; Numbers 14:18; Deuteronomy 4:31; Nehemiah 9:17; Psalm 103:8; 145:8; Joel 2:13; Jonah 4:2; and Nahum 1:3.

32 Singular use of word is for grammatical harmony with a singular person doing the speaking. Cf. MacArthur, *1 Corinthians,* 373.

some, at most two or three, to speak in tongues so that someone could hear the mighty works of God in their own language. If this is what Paul has in mind then the purpose of a translation is to build up those who do not speak the language that was spoken, so that they can understand what was said and know that God is a God of order.

Given the immense emphasis Paul has placed on understandable words and words that instruct, we must ask ourselves if tongues are appropriate during a worship service in which all in attendance speak the same language? It is my conviction that tongues would not be appropriate in this context because they would not fit the design and purpose of this gift.

If all who are gathered together speak the same language, there is no need for another language to be spoken, everyone is already capable of hearing and understanding what is being taught or prophesied. So how then should the spiritual gift of tongues, and interpretation thereof, be utilized by believers today?

First, the Holy Spirit may empower this gift within a setting where non-believers are present and there is a language barrier. The speaking of a known language that is unknown to the speaker may be used to communicate the mighty works of God to someone who may not otherwise hear and understand. One example that comes to mind includes those who work with ethnic groups whose languages have not been understood or written down yet. A missionary studying a people's language to communicate the gospel may be supernaturally empowered to speak a language he/she otherwise does not know.[33]

Secondly, the gift of interpretation is needed and utilized when tongues are spoken and not all in attendance know what was said. For example, if someone visits our church and only speaks Arabic, and someone is spontaneously able to speak Arabic (a known language unknown to them) and shares the gospel with them, this fits the defi-

---

33 Another hypothetical example that comes to mind is when my wife and I were in China. If I had been able to speak Chinese and shared the gospel with someone, that would also have been the use of this gift. This would fit with what we see in Acts 2 and does not violate Paul's instructions for the gathered church in 1 Corinthians 14.

nition of tongues that we have seen. Interpretation would be needed (an interpreter is required before speaking could even begin) so that everyone else who does not speak Arabic would know what was said.

Another example may also include a Holy Spirit-empowered ability to understand and translate known languages that are unknown to the listener or interpreter. Again, someone working with people groups whose language is not written down or codified may possibly experience this gift.

God has given his church the spiritual gifts of tongues and the interpretation of tongues. Admittedly though, the definition and examples given in this book present a limited experience for this gift in today's church. While not intending to limit the ability of the Holy Spirit to do whatever he pleases, there are many contexts and situations where tongues do not fit the definition or purpose outlined in Scripture. Moreover, what we see and hear claimed within today's charismatic and Pentecostal churches is not even in the ballpark of what Paul instructs and describes in 1 Corinthians 12–14.

The list of spiritual gifts in 1 Corinthians 12 is not exhaustive, for as we shall see there are other passages in which other gifts are mentioned and commended to the church. However, the list of spiritual gifts in 1 Corinthians 12 is the most hotly debated list of gifts. What has been written thus far is intended to be a biblically faithful and viable option for those who cannot be cessationists, but also cannot identify themselves with the modern-day charismatic or Pentecostal theological convictions.

13

SPIRITUAL GIFTS IN
1 CORINTHIANS 12:28-31

By the time we arrive at 1 Corinthians 12:28–31, we have learned several things:

1. Only those who confess that Jesus is Lord are truly spiritual people (12:3).
2. Different spiritual gifts are given and used in different places with different results, but God equally empowers them all in everyone (12:4–6).
3. Everyone in the body of Christ has been given a spiritual gift for the common good (12:7).
4. All spiritual gifts are empowered by one and the same Spirit who does so as He wills (12:11).
5. Believers are a body together and have been equally baptized into the body of Christ by the Holy Spirit. There does not exist a hierarchy of spiritual people (12:13).
6. It is wrong to conclude that I am less important than someone else if I don't like the part of the body that God has chosen for me (12:14–20).
7. It is wrong to conclude that someone else is less important than me if God has made them a different part of the body (12:21–26).
8. When one part of the body suffers, the entire body suffers (12:27).

These truths are significant as we continue to think about how spiritual gifts are intended to function within the body. Throughout 1 Corinthians 12, Paul's overwhelming emphasis and instruction is about living as a body with one another. This must not be lost on us. Furthermore, it is these truths that set the context for 1 Corinthians 14, and why Paul prohibits worship/prayer language as a legitimate use for speaking in tongues.

As we get to 1 Corinthians 12:28, we are immediately faced with another interpretive challenge. Here, for the first time in this context, Paul introduces apostles, prophets, and teachers into the mix, and appears to add them to another listing of spiritual gifts. What is more, the way Paul introduces apostles, prophets, and teachers, using first, second, third, suggests that he is elevating these three positions within the church! As a result, these verses become another significant place of disagreement between theologians.

Questions regarding whether the apostles and prophets spoken of here are offices or giftings matter greatly. For if Paul is speaking of offices, then we must determine if Paul is indicating that there is an enduring apostolic authority today, or if his reference to the office of Apostle is limited to the original men commissioned by Christ. Or perhaps, Paul is referring to a lowercase "a" apostle who has the spiritual gift of church planting and taking the gospel to new places.

The position held by those within the NAR is that Paul speaks of offices and that these offices continue for the church today. Advocating that perspective, Danny Silk writes in his book *Culture of Honor,* "…the Church needs to be founded upon leaders who carry a primary core value for the supernatural. Rather than having the apostle and prophet at the foundation of church culture, today the American church has largely placed the teacher, pastor, or evangelist at the helm. But effectively divorcing the supernatural from ministry in this way has drastically impacted the general understanding of the true role of each anointing."[1]

In *Apostles and Prophets*, Peter Wagner outlines a major distinctive of NAR theology and practice. He firmly believes there are still

---

1 Silk, *Culture of Honor,* Loc. 563, Kindle.

apostles today that operate with the same level of authority as within the New Testament. He states, "Until recently the central focus of authority in our churches existed in groups, not individuals. Trust has been placed in sessions, consistories, nominating committees, deacon boards, trustees, congregations, presbyteries, associations, general councils, cabinets, conventions, synods and the like. Rarely has trust for ultimate decision making been given to individuals such as pastors or apostles. This, however, is changing decisively in the New Apostolic Reformation."[2] Critiquing the NAR, Geivett and Pivec write,

> The main NAR teaching about apostles, which sets the movement apart from the views of other Christians, is that they must govern the church. By govern, we mean that they direct the church in an authoritative way.
>
> NAR apostles claim they hold a formal office in church government like that office of pastor or elder. Except the apostle's office wields much more authority than these other offices because an apostle has a jurisdiction over multiple churches and not mere oversight of a single church. And an apostle's authority can extend beyond churches to cities and workplaces, and among institutions that have no connection with the church.
>
> Many NAR leaders teach that apostles hold the most important office in the church. They are the equivalent of generals. All other church leaders in what they call their apostolic network—including pastors—are expected to submit to the apostle's authority.
>
> In contrast to this novel and revolutionary NAR view of apostles, Protestant Christians typically don't believe that contemporary apostles must govern churches. They believe instead that the governing office of apostle was a temporary

---

2 Wagner, *Apostles*. 25

office in the early church held by a special class of apostles—those appointed directly by the resurrected Lord and including the Twelve and Paul.[3]

What exactly does the word apostle mean, and how is Paul using the word in 1 Corinthians 12:28? Is Paul speaking of an office or a gifting? If an office, does this office endure, or has it stopped? It is to these questions we next turn our attention.

Apostles

The word apostle (ἀπόστολος) is used in the New Testament 80 times in 79 verses and is defined by BDAG as "messengers with or without extraordinary status."[4] The TDNT adds, "in the NT ἀπόστολος never means the act of sending, or figuratively the object of sending. It always denotes a man who is sent and sent with full authority."[5] In classical Greek the word was used in reference "to sea-faring, and more particularly to military expeditions ... in this way it comes to be applied on the one side to a group of men sent out for a particular purpose, e.g., not merely to an army but to a band of colonists and their settlement."[6]

In the Gospels, Matthew, Mark, and John use this word collectively four times.[7] Matthew and Mark both directly refer to the men Jesus selected as Apostles, and John quotes Jesus as he gives final instructions to his Apostles, in part telling them that a "*messenger* is not greater than the one who sent him" (John 13:16).

In Luke's gospel account he uses the word six times, and in each occurrence his direct reference is to the 12 men that Jesus selected and appointed as Apostles.[8] In the book of Acts, Luke uses the word *apostles* 30 times and every time he uses this word, save one, he is directly referring to those called and commissioned by Christ, minus

---

3 Geivett and Pivec, *God's Super-Apostles*, 8.

4 BDAG, 122.

5 TDNT, 421.

6 BDAG, 122; TDNT, 407.

7 Matt. 10:2, Mark 3:14, 6:30, John 13:16

8 At this point, including Judas.

Judas, plus Matthias and Paul.[9] The one occurrence where Luke uses the word *apostle* not in direct reference to one of the commissioned Apostles or Paul is in Acts 14:14 where Barnabas and Paul are both listed as Apostles.[10]

The commissioning of the Apostles occurred during the ministry of Jesus while he was on earth and the Gospel writers record for us that the 12 men Jesus appointed were the men He named as Apostles.[11] As we read in Acts 1, Matthias, along with Joseph/Barsabbas/Justus, had been a witness to the life and ministry of Christ but they had not been divinely commissioned by Christ as the others had been. The purpose of casting lots then was twofold: (1) to identify for the others who the Lord had "chosen to take the place in this ministry and apostle-ship from which Judas turned aside" (Acts 1:24–25), and (2) divinely commission who the Lord had chosen.

Of tremendous importance is what Luke records in Acts 1 regarding the replacement of Judas, for there we see the criteria the other Apostles used in determining who should be considered an Apostle with them. In Acts 1:21–22 Luke writes, "So one of the men who have accompanied us during all the time that the Lord Jesus went in and out among us, beginning from the baptism of John until the day when he was taken up from us—one of these men must become with us a witness to his resurrection."

Here we read that an Apostle was to be one who had accompanied the other men during Jesus's earthly ministry. He was to have witnessed firsthand the things Jesus did and said. Following Peter's instructions, the group put forward two men: Joseph/Barsabbas/Justus and Matthias. They then prayed and cast lots for who should take Judas's place. The lots fell to Matthias.

---

9 Incidentally, the last time Luke uses the word *apostles* is in Acts 16:4 when he is referring to what happened at the Jerusalem Council. Like we saw with his usage of *signs and wonders*, once again after this pivotal moment in the early church this word is no longer recorded in Scripture. Two of these occurrences, 5:34 and 15:33, are found in some manuscripts/translations and not others.

10 It is indeed possible that Christ commissioned Barnabas like he did Matthias, but we do not have any record of such an event happening.

11 Matthew 10:2; Mark 3:14, 6:30; Luke 6:13.

TO EACH IS GIVEN

The New Testament also gives us one other qualification for someone to be called an Apostle. Grudem helpfully summarizes that they must be "specifically commissioned by Christ as his apostle."[12] Thus the two qualifications that must be met to be considered an Apostle on par with those originally chosen by Jesus are (1) witnessing Christ's life and resurrection and (2) being commissioned by Christ himself as an Apostle.

The Apostle Paul made much of the fact that he was a witness to the ministry of Jesus, and that he had also received a divine commissioning. Even though the means of Paul's witness was certainly different than the others, he makes it clear that the Lord appeared to him. In 1 Corinthians 15:8–9, he writes, "Last of all, as to one untimely born, he appeared also to me. For I am the least of the apostles, unworthy to be called an apostle, because I persecuted the church of God."

Furthermore, in defending his status as an Apostle earlier in 1 Corinthians 9:1 Paul writes, "Am I not an apostle? Have I not seen Jesus our Lord?" In Galatians 1 Paul also states that he did not receive the gospel from any man but rather "received it through a revelation of Jesus Christ." This more than likely occurred during his three years in Arabia (v. 17).

Regarding his divine commissioning as an Apostle, Paul, in speaking before Agrippa, states in Acts 26:16–18 that Christ spoke to him and said,

> But rise and stand upon your feet, for I have appeared to you for this purpose, to appoint you as a servant and witness to the things in which you have seen me and to those in which I will appear to you, delivering you from your people and from the Gentiles—to whom I am sending you to open their eyes, so that they may turn from darkness to light and from the power of Satan to God, that they may receive forgiveness of sins and a place among those who are sanctified by faith in me.

---

12 Grudem, *Systematic Theology*, 906.

Therefore, even though Paul was not one of the original 12 who were appointed and commissioned by Christ, he does indeed meet the qualifications that the other 12 met. Paul is a legitimate Apostle and selected by God as such for this distinct purpose.

In his letters, Paul uses the word *apostle* 34 times in 33 different verses, and his use of the word, by and large, reflects the exact way Luke uses the word *Apostle* in the book of Acts. However, Paul does not exclusively use the word a*postle* in this way.

Throughout Paul's writings there are several instances where he uses the word *apostle(s)* and is not referring to the original commissioned Apostles or himself. As we consider what Paul means by his use of the word apostle in 1 Corinthians 12, we need to think through the instances where he does not specifically refer to an Apostle who meets both qualifications. What follows is a summary and brief explanation of these instances:

1. His references to "super-apostles,"[13]

2. His references to Epaphroditus and other brothers who are apostles/messengers,[14]

3. His reference to James, the brother of Jesus,[15]

4. His potential reference to Andronicus and Junia (Junias) as ones well-known to the apostles, and[16]

5. His use of the word *apostle* in Ephesians 4 to refer to gifted individuals who do not occupy the office of Apostle.[17]

In 2 Corinthians 11:5, 13, and 12:11, no serious consideration is given to Paul equating the super-apostles with true Apostles. In fact, the entire point he is making while defending himself to the Corinthians is that he is not like these super-apostles who are false apostles and de-

---

13 2 Cor. 11:5, 13; 12:11.

14 Phil. 2:25; 2 Cor. 8:23.

15 Gal. 1:19.

16 Rom. 16:7.

17 A detailed argument of this interpretation is given below.

ceitful workmen. Thus, Paul's use of the word *apostles* in 2 Corinthians 11 and 12 does correspond to the original 12 and himself through the contrast he draws between true Apostles and false apostles.

In 2 Corinthians 8:23, Paul refers to *our brothers* who are apostles (messengers) of the church and in Philippians 2:25 Paul refers to Epaphroditus as an apostle (messenger) for the Philippians and minister to Paul's needs. In both instances, the word *apostle* is rendered as *messenger* in our English Bibles to help avoid confusion and to signify that Paul was not referring to Epaphroditus, or the other brothers as Apostles, but rather those who were sent out as authorized messengers.[18]

In the technical sense of the word, Paul's use of the word *apostle* makes sense.[19] These *other brothers* that Paul refers to are indeed capable of being authorized messengers sent out for the proclamation of the gospel. In the theological sense of the word, it is helpful that our English translations provide a distinction.

In Galatians 1:19, Paul writes, "But I saw none of the other apostles except James the Lord's brother." Unfortunately, we have no record of James being commissioned by his half-brother Jesus to be an Apostle. However, given the favorable way Paul writes about James, and Paul's clear understanding of what it meant to be appointed and called as an Apostle, it is reasonable for us to conclude that James was an Apostle in the sense that Peter, Paul, and the other 11 were.

Perhaps the most challenging passage, grammatically, is Romans 16:7. In this passage, Paul uses the word *apostle*, alongside the unknown gender of Junia (Junias) and with a prepositional phrase that can mean, *to the apostles* or *among the apostles*. Thus, we must determine first if Paul's prepositional phrase is indicating that the Apostles have knowledge of Andronicus and Junia (Junias) or if these two

---

18 Because of the lack of any names, except for Titus who Paul does not include in the "brothers," it is entirely possible that Paul is referring to other brothers who were a part of the 12 apostles. We simply do not know one way or another who he is referring to exactly.

19 Epaphroditus was indeed an authorized and sent messenger from the Philippian church to Paul. In this way he was indeed their apostle to Paul.

individuals were known among the Apostles in the sense that they belonged to the same group.

The preposition translated *to* in the ESV and *among* in the NASB95 and NIV is the Greek word ἐν and is best translated in this context as *among* as the NASB95 and NIV have. Thomas Schreiner writes regarding this phrase that "The consensus view is that the phrase means 'distinguished among the apostles' ... In saying that they are apostles, however, Paul is certainly not placing them in the ranks of the Twelve."[20] Thus, as he does with the *other brothers* in 2 Corinthians 8, and Epaphroditus in Philippians 2, Paul is identifying Andronicus and Junia (Junias) as those who are authorized messengers of the gospel, but not those divinely commissioned as Apostles.

Regarding the gender of Junia (Junias), Schreiner also helpfully points out that "most recent commentaries on Romans ... favor the feminine [Junia] since the contracted form of Junianus is nowhere found in Greek literature. Moreover, the majority opinion by far until at least the thirteenth century was that the person in question was a woman—Junia."[21] Consequently, in Romans 16:7, we likely have a direct reference to an authorized messenger of the gospel, who had been "in Christ before" Paul, being a woman!

To begin synthesizing the biblical data regarding the word *apostle,* it may be helpful for us to think of this word in the sense of two categories: office and gifting; or in the words of Grudem, "narrow and broad." Regarding how to best understand the word *apostle* Grudem writes, "The word *apostle* can be used in a broad or narrow sense. In a broad sense, it just means 'messenger' or 'pioneer missionary.' But in a narrow sense, the most common sense in the New Testament, it refers to a specific office, 'apostle of Jesus Christ.'"[22]

The office of Apostle is occupied by those who meet the qualifications for Apostle that the Twelve, Matthias, and Paul all meet.

---

20 Thomas Schreiner, *Romans,* (Grand Rapids: Baker Academic, 2003), 79.

21 Ibid., 796.

22 Grudem, *Systematic Theology,* 911. Applying Grudem's breakdown to this book yields the distinction: Apostle=narrow and apostle=broad.

To Each Is Given

Because this is an office with specific qualifications and functions, we can affirm the unique, foundational, role of the Apostles within the early church, which included the performing of signs and wonders, and authoring of Scripture. And because of the qualifications that these Apostles had to meet, this office ceased to exist when the Apostle John died sometime after penning the book of Revelation. Therefore, it is unbiblical to assert that the office of Apostle continues today.

The gifting of apostle, however, can be given by God to those who did not meet the qualifications of the Apostles but are nonetheless sent out to proclaim the gospel as authorized messengers. In this sense, we can understand, for example, church planters, and missionaries as those with the gifting of apostle.[23] The differences between office and gifting lie fundamentally with the authority of the one sending and the level of authority the one sent is given.

Regarding the authority of the one sending, think of the President of the United States sending a messenger or delegate to a meeting of the United Nations and the *New York Times* sending a reporter (delegate) to the very same meeting. Both individuals are at the United Nations representing the ones who sent them. However, there is a distinct difference in the role of each because of the authority of the sender. Similarly, Epaphroditus being sent by Paul to the Philippians (Phil. 2:25) is not the same as Jesus commissioning Paul to go to the Gentiles (Gal. 1:14–16).

Regarding the level of authority the sent one has, another illustration may be helpful. Every summer the Charis Fellowship hosts a national conference and churches from within the Fellowship are given the opportunity to send delegates to vote at the annual business meeting. The church I pastor is given three delegate votes at this meeting regardless of how many people we may send to the national conference. If, for example, we send five people to conference, three

---

23 See chapter 16.

of them have a different level of authority than the remaining two. Only three are allowed to officially represent our church at the ballot box, and yet all five were sent by our church.

Jesus called and commissioned a limited group of individuals to occupy the office of Apostle. However, he gifts men and women today as apostles. While the authority of Jesus has never changed, the authority He gives the ones He gifts has. Consequently, the office has ceased, while the gift continues today.[24]

What we have observed thus far through the Gospels, Acts, and Paul's writing is that the term *apostle* is used most frequently to refer to those men who have been appointed, called, and commissioned by Christ to proclaim the gospel. However, Paul does not use *apostle* exclusively to refer to just these men, he also uses the word apostle to refer to *other brothers*, Epaphroditus, Andronicus, and Junia.

At this point in the discussion it is reasonable to conclude that when the Apostle Paul uses *apostle,* he normally has in mind the appointed, called, and commissioned leaders that Christ appointed, and if he intends to use the word differently that intent becomes clear with the context.

Returning to 1 Corinthians 12, it is my conviction that Paul is writing of the specific group of Apostles that witnessed the life and ministry of Jesus and were specifically commissioned by Him to be His authorized messengers. As Garland succinctly puts it, "'Apostles' refers to the witnesses of the resurrection who were especially called out by God and appear to be a closed circle."[25] This conclusion is based on Paul's use of the word *apostle* throughout his writings and his use of the ordinal number "first," and the greater point that Paul is making in 1 Corinthians regarding the body of Christ.[26]

---

24 See chapter 17.

25 Garland, *1 Corinthians,* 599.

26 Admittedly, there are many interpretations regarding whether this is an office or gift. The one I offer has some, although not tremendously strong, exegetical support. In this sense, it is more of a theological and contextual conclusion.

To Each Is Given

In the context of 1 Corinthians 12, Paul's point in bringing up Apostles is not to speak to an enduring office but rather to distinguish between different parts of the body that have different functions. This interpretation is supported by Paul's rhetorical question in verse 29, "Are all Apostles?" The obvious answer is no, and that is Paul's point. The body has different parts that function differently, and this is by the design of its Creator, just like our physical bodies.

What must be asked next is whether this interpretation holds for both prophets and teachers. If not, then the conclusion offered regarding *Apostle* would suffer from the logical fallacy of special pleading and therein must be rejected. However, if it does hold for prophets and teachers, then we may find further confirmation within this difficult set of verses.

Prophets

The Greek word *prophets* is προφήτης and is defined as "a person inspired to proclaim or reveal divine will or purpose."[27] The TDNT defines this word as "normally a biblical proclaimer of a divinely inspired message ... not a magician or soothsayer."[28] *Prophet* is used 144 times in the New Testament, and there is no dispute that it normally refers to the Old Testament prophets who wrote and spoke as God commanded them. Nevertheless, while this is the predominant way *prophet* is used in the New Testament, it is not the only way the term is used.

If we do not consider John the Baptist or Jesus, who were both called prophets,[29] we are left with the following instances where the word *prophet* is used to describe someone other than an Old Testament prophet.

Luke 2:36
"And there was a prophetess, Anna, the daughter of Phanuel, of the tribe of Asher. She was advanced in years, having lived with her husband seven years from when she was a virgin..."

---

27 BDAG, 890.

28 TDNT, 960.

29 Matt. 11:9 (John the Baptist); John 4:19 (Jesus).

Acts 11:27

"Now in these days prophets came down from Jerusalem to Antioch."

Acts 13:1

"Now there were in the church at Antioch prophets and teachers, Barnabas, Simeon who was called Niger, Lucius of Cyrene, Manaen a lifelong friend of Herod the tetrarch, and Saul."

Acts 15:32

"And Judas and Silas, who were themselves prophets, encouraged and strengthened the brothers with many words."

Acts 21:10

"While we were staying for many days, a prophet named Agabus came down from Judea."

1 Corinthians 14:29

"Let two or three prophets speak, and let the others weigh what is said."

1 Corinthians 14:32

"... and the spirits of prophets are subject to prophets."

1 Corinthians 14:37

"If anyone thinks that he is a prophet, or spiritual, he should acknowledge that the things I am writing to you are a command of the Lord."

Titus 1:12

"One of the Cretans, a prophet of their own, said, 'Cretans are always liars, evil beasts, lazy gluttons.'"

As we look at these passages, we must admit that someone other than an Old Testament level prophet is the exception rather than the norm. One cannot simply claim that nine occurrences out of 144 is anything other than an exception. Nonetheless, the exception does exist and we must not ignore it. Regarding what these individuals did as prophets (and we could include here Philip's daughters who are said to prophesy, but not called prophetesses),[30] it appears they spoke messages

---

30 Acts 21:9.

from God that did not have the weight or authority of Scripture. The most interesting of these prophets is Agabus. [31]

Agabus appears twice in the New Testament, once in Acts 11 and once in Acts 21. In Acts 11 his prophecy brought about immediate action on the part of the disciples. In response to his prophecy regarding a famine, we are told they [the disciples] "determined, everyone according to his ability, to send relief to the brothers living in Judea. And they did so, sending it to the elders by the hand of Barnabas and Saul (vv. 29-20)."

In Acts 21:10, Agabus shows up again and has another prophecy, from the Spirit, that "the Jews in Jerusalem will bind the man who owns this belt and deliver him into the hands of the Gentiles." In response to this prophecy, those with Paul urged him, "not to go up to Jerusalem" (v. 12). Also, earlier Luke writes, "And having sought out the disciples, we stayed there for seven days. And through the Spirit they were telling Paul not to go to Jerusalem" (v. 4). Furthermore, while there is no direct record of what Philip's daughters prophesied, it is likely, based on the context of what Luke is recording, that they also were urging Paul not to go to Jerusalem. But, Paul "would not be persuaded" (v. 14).

How then is Paul able to disobey those who "through the Spirit were telling him not to go on to Jerusalem?"[32] The answer lies in the fact that these prophets and prophecies were not on par with the prophets from the Old Testament, nor the Old Testament itself which was commonly referred to as the Law and the Prophets.

This reality is one of the most striking aspects regarding the use of the word *prophet* in the New Testament when it is not referring directly to an Old Testament prophet or the Old Testament Scriptures.

---

31 Whether all who have the spiritual gift of prophecy should be called prophets is not a question directly answered by the Scriptures, though Paul does refer to them as such in 1 Cor. 14. However, based on how the word *prophets* is predominantly used in the New Testament and the claim by certain charismatic and Pentecostal groups that the office of prophet still exists, it seems wise to not call any one person a prophet. To state that a person has the spiritual gift of prophecy would be preferable.
32 Acts 21:4.

When referring directly to the Old Testament Scriptures or its authors, obedience is expected, and disobedience is condemned because an authoritative word from the Lord has been given. However, while these other prophecies were indeed from the Lord, through his Spirit, they did not carry the same level of authority as Scripture.

In summary, the New Testament *prophet* refers to the authors of the Old Testament or what was written by them. A few exceptions do exist where this word refers to individuals other than Old Testament prophets, but their prophetic words were not considered authoritative and obedience to them was not required. As we concluded with apostle regarding office and gifting, it is also helpful to understand that there was an office of prophet and a gifting of prophecy.

It appears best to interpret Paul's use of the word *prophet* in 1 Corinthians 12:28 as referring to those who occupied the Old Testament office of prophet. For the same reasons as given regarding *apostle*, I believe Paul is writing about a specific group of individuals who were used by the Lord to lay the foundation of the church. Although chronologically these men came before the apostles, Paul places them second in importance in his list—something he also does twice in the book of Ephesians.[33]

Teachers

The third office that Paul speaks of is teacher (διδάσκαλος). The noun *teacher* appears in the New Testament 59 times and is simply defined as teacher and primarily refers to Jesus, though others are called teachers in the New Testament.[34] The TDNT adds, "The teacher here is one who expounds the divine will as laid down in Scripture. When the term is applied to others such as John the Baptist or Nicodemus, it consistently means a person who indicates the way of God from the law."[35] Significant for our purposes is the fact that teachers teach the Scriptures. They expound on what God has revealed and provide instructions to their students.

---

33 Eph. 2:20, 3:5.

34 BDAG, 241.

35 TDNT, 164.

To Each Is Given

The verb teach (διδάσκω) appears in the New Testament 97 times in 91 different verses and is defined as "to tell someone what to do, and to provide instruction in a formal or informal setting."[36] Of these 97 occurrences, 58 happen in the Gospel accounts of Jesus's life. Throughout Matthew, Mark, Luke, and John, this word almost exclusively refers to the ministry of Jesus and his actions as a teacher. Out of the 55 times this word appears, only nine occurrences refer to someone other than Jesus. If you include references to the Father and the Holy Spirit, then only six of 55 occurrences refer to someone other than a member of the Trinity.

Also related to the noun teacher is the adjective *able to teach* (διδακτικόν), which is a unique qualification that all elders must meet. Appearing only twice in the New Testament this adjective is used once in reference to elders (1 Tim. 3:2), and once in reference to the *Lord's servant* (2 Tim. 2:24) which immediately applies to Timothy and more broadly applies to all others who occupy a position of leadership within the church as Timothy did.

Once again, as we saw with apostle and prophet, it is best to interpret Paul as writing about specific offices that occur within the church and not those with the spiritual gift of teaching. However, unlike the offices of Apostle and Prophet, the office of Teacher continues today, through the office of elder, and is vitally important for the church. God has given the body of Christ teachers to teach God's revealed Word so that the body may be built up in sound doctrine and equipped for ministry, and while all teachers do not have to be elders, all elders must be able to teach.

Not only does the office interpretation fit with the context of 1 Corinthians 12:28–30, it also allows us to understand Paul's prohibition of women teaching "or exercising authority over a man" (1 Tim. 2:12) because those are functions of the office of elder/teacher. However, we can equally affirm the spiritual gift of teaching found in Romans 12:7 and Ephesians 4:11 as available to both men and women as God assigns.

---

36 BDAG, 241.

By interpreting Paul's use of the ordinal numbers (i.e. first, second, and third) for the grammatical purpose of highlighting three important offices within the church, when we arrive at the next item in the list, we are able to see that Paul shifts back to a listing of spiritual gifts.

The Remaining Gifts in 1 Cor. 12

Continuing in verse 28, Paul next writes about miracles, gifts of healings, helping, administration, and various kinds of tongues. Because this list contains two spiritual gifts that Paul does not list in verses 8–10, we are once again reminded that no list of spiritual gifts in the Bible is complete or comprehensive.[37]

Helping (ἀντιλήμψεις)—Those gifted with the ability or capacity to assist.[38] This word is used one time in the New Testament, and those with the spiritual gift of helping are supernaturally empowered by the Holy Spirit to serve in a variety of ways.

Administrating (κυβερνήσεις)—Those gifted to lead.[39] This word also occurs only one time in the New Testament and is related to the Greek word κυβερνάω, which means one who is responsible for the management of a ship.[40] The idea this word calls to mind is of a ship captain who guides the ship to its intended destination. In similar ways, God has gifted individuals within his church with the Holy Spirit-empowered ability to lead and guide.

In verses 29–30, Paul begins to summarize the main point of chapter 12 and does so by asking seven rhetorical questions that all anticipate the answer no. The point he makes could not be any clearer. Not everyone in the church is an Apostle; not everyone has been given the gift of tongues; not everyone has an utterance of wisdom. However, everyone has been given a manifestation of the Spirit for the common good. There exists no hierarchy of importance within the body, and while it is true that the Apostles had a unique role in the early church,

---

37 For miracles, gifts of healings, and various kinds of tongues see above.

38 BDAG, 89.

39 BDAG, 573.

40 BDAG, 574 (Rev. 18:17).

they were no more chosen, arranged, or appointed by God than anyone else in the body.

Finally, verse 31 serves as a reminder of the Corinthians' error and is the hinge verse between chapters 12 and 13. The verb *desire*, translated in most English versions as a command, can also be translated as an indicative verb.[41] Fee notes, "It is possible to read the verb as an indicative ... [though] what basically stands against this option is the twofold later appearance of the same verb form, where it can be only an imperative and not an indicative."[42]

However, even if we conclude, as every major English translation does, that the word *desire* is best translated as an imperative command we should not miss the adjective *higher* that Paul uses to modify the gifts he speaks of. BDAG defines *higher* (μέγας) as "pertaining to being relatively superior in importance."[43] Ciampa and Rosner note,

> Thiselton provides the best explanation of this part of the verse and how it relates to the Corinthians' issues. They had demonstrated a "zealous concern, even a striving, for the gifts of the Spirit that were deemed to be greatest in the sense of their supposedly constituting a mark of a high social and/or spiritual status." But Paul redefines the terms since he completely rejects the Corinthians' approach to deciding what counts as high spiritual status and the way gifts relates to such status. Ironically, he urges them, "Do not stop being zealously concerned about the 'greatest' gifts, provided that you follow me in transposing and subverting your understanding of what counts as 'the greatest.'"[44]

In this sense, *higher* would not be a distinction between the individual gifts that Paul has listed, but a correction to the Corinthian error of

---

41 A grammatical interpretation of the Greek construction allows for, which would fit Paul's main point in chapter 12 and serve as a transition into chapter 13.

42 Fee, *Epistle to the Corinthians,* 690–691.

43 BDAG, 624.

44 Ciampa and Rosner, *The First Letter to the Corinthians,* 616.

believing that some gifts or people were of greater significance than other gifts. Even if we interpret verse 31 as a command, we still must recognize that God has a very different definition of gifts and people than the Corinthians do, which comes as no surprise because this has been a sustained theme throughout the entire letter.

The main point of chapter 12 is to correct the error of the Corinthian church that some people were more spiritual, and thus more important than others. As noted, earlier Paul's extensive use of words to communicate God's sovereignty in gifting and composing the body is for the express purpose of correcting this error. As he shifts into chapter 13, Paul now tells them that he is going to show them a better way. The way of love.

14

SPIRITUAL GIFTS
IN OTHER PASSAGES:
ROMANS 12 AND 1 PETER 4

First Corinthians is not the only book in Scripture that outlines the different spiritual gifts that believers are given. It is, however, the book that usually gets the most attention because of the reference to tongues and interpretation of tongues. Nevertheless, the gifts listed in Romans 12, 1 Peter 4, and Ephesians 4 are just as important to the body of Christ as the gifts listed in 1 Corinthians 12. As we move from 1 Corinthians 12 to these other passages, we will again seek to define the gifts that Paul and Peter list.[1]

Before we define the gifts listed in Romans 12:6, we need first to consider what the Apostle Paul says in verses 3–5, for in doing so we are once again reminded of how we ought to think of ourselves (and our gifts) in relation to others within the body of Christ. In short, there is no room for pride. The Apostle writes, "For by the grace given to me I say to everyone among you not to think of himself more highly than he ought to think, but to think with sober judgment, each according to the measure of faith that God has assigned. For as in one body we have many members, and the members do not all have the same function, so we, though many, are one body in Christ, and individually members one of another."

Having just instructed this church to "present their bodies as living sacrifices" (v. 12:1) and to "not be conformed to this world" (v. 12:2) Paul now begins providing examples of how they might apply his

---

1 Where there is an overlap from one list to another the prior definition will be either given or referenced.

instructions to their everyday lives, beginning first with their relationship with one another.

Without question, the sin of pride is often clearly seen among those who are conformed to the world. World and national leaders speak and act with hubris, often regarding other people as either persons they can use to accomplish their own desires or individuals to be conquered and trampled upon. This, however, is not to be the mindset of those within the church. Believers are to think differently and in doing so recognize that they are just one of a myriad of body parts—all of which are needed.

One interesting aspect of verse 3 is that the word Paul uses, which we translate *think of himself more highly* (ὑπερφρονεῖν), appears to have been created by Paul for this very sentence. It is only used once in the entire New Testament and is a compound word meaning to "think too highly of oneself, be haughty."[2] Not only that, but there is another compound verb present in this verse as well. It is the word *sober* (σωφρονέω) which BDAG defines as "to be prudent, with focus on self-control."[3] Furthermore, Paul uses these two compound verbs to bookend two other present active verbs that are translated as *think* (φρονέω), creating a play on words within the text. Schriener writes, "Believers are not to be proud but to have a sober, sane, sensible, and realistic estimate of themselves."[4] We are to continually demonstrate humility toward one another, not hubris.

The rationale that Paul provides for why believers are to act this way is first grounded in the sovereignty of God. As was noted in 1 Corinthians 12 regarding God's sovereign composition of the body of Christ, the same truth emerges here. We are to continually think with humble, sober judgment, about ourselves and one another because of the measure of faith that God has assigned.

The word *assigned* (ἐμέρισεν) is defined as "to make an allotment, deal out, apportion"[5] and communicates that God has determined the

---

2 BDAG, 1034.

3 BDAG, 986.

4 Schreiner, *Romans,* 652.

5 BDAG, 632.

type of role/part that one will play within his body. Yet, despite having differing roles and functions, all believers are a part of one body, according to the measure of faith that God has given to each. In his commentary on Romans, John Murray notes, "They have property in one another and therefore in one another's gifts and graces. This is not the communism which destroys personal property; it is community that recognizes the distinguishing gifts which God has distributed."[6] Therefore, our continual thinking about ourselves and others must not be conformed to the world but rather transformed by the renewing of our minds (v. 1).

God wants us, as his children, to think differently about ourselves and one another than our world thinks. While gifts vary in function, all individual parts of the body are members with one another.

Gifts in Romans 12

Prophecy (προφητεία)—See above definition of prophecy.

Service (διακονία)—Those gifted at serving as an attendant, aide, or assistant.[7] This word is closely related to the word deacon, and this spiritual gift empowers men and women to serve and help.

Teaching (διδάσκω)—Those gifted at "the act of teaching."[8] This gift can be given to either men or women, and the use of this gift has nothing to do with the size or age of the audience.

Exhortation (παρακαλέω)—Those gifted "to instill someone with courage or cheer,"[9] to passionately encourage the body toward obedience and submission to the Lordship of Christ. It includes both the call to repentance from sin and the encouragement and comfort of discouraged believers.[10]

---

6 John Murray, *The Epistle to the Romans* (Grand Rapids MI: Eerdmans Publishing 1993), 120.

7 BDAG, 230.

8 Ibid., 240.

9 Ibid., 765.

10 The "act of emboldening another in belief or course of action," BDAG, 766; LN, 25.150. In 1 Tim. 3:4, 5, 12 Paul uses this word in relation to one's home as a qualification that elders and deacons must meet in order to serve in those roles.

TO EACH IS GIVEN

Generosity (ἁπλότης)—Those gifted to generously, or liberally, share their resources with others.[11]

Leadership (προίστημι)—Those gifted to exercise a position of leadership."[12] Causing people to follow them to a recommended course of action.

Mercy (ἐλεάω)—Those gifted by the Holy Spirit to show kindness or concern for someone in need.[13]

Gifts in 1 Peter 4

The list of spiritual gifts that Peter gives in 1 Peter 4:10–11 is more a list of spiritual gift categories than specific gifts. In fact, we can easily take each of the gifts the Apostle Paul lists and place them within one of the two categories that Peter gives. This is not in any way meant to dismiss the significance of what Peter writes, but rather to acknowledge that Peter appears to be painting in broad strokes.

Like Paul, Peter also gives instructions regarding how believers are to treat one another. In 1 Peter 4:7–9, we are to be self-controlled,[14] sober-minded;[15] loving one another earnestly for this will cover a multitude of sins. Without grumbling, we are to show hospitality to one another. Lastly, we are to serve one another as good stewards of God's varied grace.

Just as we have seen in both 1 Corinthians 12 and Romans 12, spiritual gifts are varied and given according to the sovereign choice of God. To the one who has received gifts of speaking, he or she must speak as one who speaks the oracles of God (v. 11). Those who have received gifts of serving must serve in the strength that God provides (v. 11).

Lastly, Peter provides us with a purpose clause regarding the use of these two categories of spiritual gifts. *In order that* translates the

---

11 BDAG, 104.

12 Ibid., 870.

13 Ibid., 314.

14 BDAG, 986. σωφρονέω is the same word Paul uses in Romans 12:3 that is translated sober-minded.

15 BDAG, 672 νήφω is defined as "to be prudent, with focus on self-control."

Greek word ἵνα, which indicates that Peter is telling us the purpose of these categories of gifts. God has sovereignly gifted his body with speaking and serving gifts so that God may be glorified through them.

In this chapter, we looked at the list of spiritual gifts that Paul lists in Romans 12 and the two categories of spiritual gifts that Peter identifies in his first epistle. In the next chapter, we seek to understand the list of gifts that Paul writes about in Ephesians 4.

15
SPIRITUAL GIFTS
IN OTHER PASSAGES:
EPHESIANS 4

The list of spiritual gifts in Ephesians 4 is also much-debated. On one side of the debate are those within the NAR who believe that Paul is not listing gifts but enduring offices with the same level of authority as the apostles and prophets in the Scriptures. Peter Wagner writes, "While all five offices [from Eph. 4:11] have uniquely important functions to fulfill in the life and ministry of the Church, only two are specifically designated as the *foundation* of the Church, namely apostles and prophets."[1]

Regarding this NAR teaching of Ephesians 4:11, Geivett and Pivec add, "In the NAR understanding of this passage, Jesus, at his ascension to heaven, gave the church five governing offices: apostle, prophet, evangelist, pastor (shepherd), and teacher. Verse 13, they say, clearly indicates that these five governing offices are not temporal, but ongoing because they must build up—or equip—the church *until* it reaches spiritual maturity…this NAR teaching is often referred to as the five-fold ministry teaching….Only when a church has all five offices will it become God's powerful hand to advance his kingdom."[2]

On the other side of this debate are pastors and scholars such as John MacArthur who contend that the apostles and prophets were offices that "ceased with the completion of the NT," and "were replaced

---

1 Wagner, *Apostles*, 75
2 Geivett and Pivec, *God's Super-Apostles*, 13.

by the evangelists, and teaching pastors."[3] Thus you have the list in Ephesians, like the list in 1 Corinthians 12, being broken down into offices that have ceased and gifts that still endure.[4]

Still others such as missiologists Alan Hirsch and Neil Cole, for example, see the list in Ephesians 4 as gifts to the church, not offices, and believe the use of these gifts within the church is part of the very DNA code that Jesus has written within the church.[5] Regarding what he refers to as APEST (Apostle, Prophet, Evangelist, Shepherd, Teacher), Hirsch writes, "Paul clearly states in verses 7 and 11 that Jesus 'gave' APEST to the church, distributing it among all the people as he sees fit. It is vital that you, the reader, feel the weight of the grammar that Paul uses to talk about the constitutional *givenness* of the APEST ministries to the church."[6]

Cole adds, "these five roles represent the facets of God's image that our restored humanity is intended to reflect. When these facets work together in harmony, they are what allow us to display God's glory to the nations."[7]

The challenge before us is not to reconcile all these differing interpretations, but rather interpret Ephesians 4:11 in a way that is accurate to what Paul originally intended.

Exegetically speaking, this passage is difficult and does not neatly fit with any of the other passages that we have looked at thus far. Consequently, we will first process the text as it stands by itself, and then consider some of the differences and similarities that this text has with the other spiritual gifts passages.

In chapter 4 of his letter to the church in Ephesus, the Apostle Paul shifts toward an application of the doctrine that he has just spent the

---

3 John MacArthur, *The MacArthur Bible Commentary* (Nashville: Thomas Nelson, 2005), 1693. It is interesting to note that both the NAR and MacArthur agree that "apostle and prophet" refer to offices, and not gifting, however, each group concludes something radically different from the other about the current use of these offices in the church.

4 Depending on how one interprets "shepherd and teacher."

5 Alan Hirsch, *5Q* (Columbia: 100 Movements, 2017), 4.

6 Ibid., 6.

7 Neil Cole, *Primal Fire* (Tyndale Momentum, 2014), 10.

last three chapters detailing. In verse 1, the word *therefore* alerts us to this transition and that the application he will now write is built on what he has just said. In this regard, we are reminded that doctrine is not to be separated from application, nor is application to be sought in the absence of doctrine. Rather, one flows naturally from the other and we must not only understand the profound truths of the gospel but also how those truths apply in our daily lives.

Much like we have seen in several other passages, Paul is concerned with the body of Christ being united and living in unity. As such, he first commands the Ephesians, in verse 1, to walk in a manner worthy of their calling and begins in verse 2 to explain how this command relates to their relationships with one another. With one another, they, and by extension we, are to be completely humble, gentle, and patient, bearing with one another in love and eager to maintain the unity of the Spirit. The continual pursuit of such attributes is imperative because, while there may be distinctions within the body of Christ, there is only one body of Christ.

No longer do two groups exist, Jews and Gentiles, rather, there is one new man in place of the two (Eph. 2:15). There is only one Spirit of Christ who seals and guarantees our inheritance (Eph. 1:13–14). There is only one hope, and those who once had no hope now have hope and peace in Jesus (Eph. 2:12). There is only one Lord, one faith, one baptism, and one God and Father of all (Eph. 4:4–6)!

Paul's point in verses 4–6 is that what unites them is greater than what distinguishes them. And while there may be differences within the body, those differences do not excuse a lack of unity. Rather, because of what unites us, we must walk in a manner worthy of our calling and be eager to maintain the unity of the Spirit.

Against this backdrop, Paul then moves to highlight some of the differences within the church.[8] In verse 7 we are told, "But grace was given to each one of us according to the measure of Christ's gift."

---

8 These are both external, namely ethnic, differences as well as differences regarding spiritual giftings. Principally this can and should also apply to all external differences in the church. Some ready examples that come to mind are political preferences, "dress codes," schooling choices, parenting styles, and musical tastes, etc.

TO EACH IS GIVEN

In verse 7, we first need to acknowledge the use of the conjunction *but* (δέ) which is connecting verse 7 to the preceding verses and yet indicating that a mild contrast is forthcoming. BDAG defines this word as "a marker with an additive relation, with possible suggestion of contrast"[9] Here, Paul is commanding them to pursue unity within the body of Christ over against the reality that distinctions exist within the body of Christ. What is more, these distinctions are not surface level or mere human distinctions, these distinctions exist according to the measure of Christ's gift.

The word *given* in verse 7 is the Greek word δίδωμι and has a wide range of meaning.[10] Throughout the New Testament, this word is used frequently; 415 times in 378 verses, and here it appears to carry with it the simple meaning of *give* that comes most naturally to mind.

Related to this word is the noun *gift* (δωρεά); which is what Paul indicates Christ has given. BDAG defines the word *gift* as "that which is given or transferred freely by one person to another.[11] Both the verb *given* and the noun *gift* come from the same root word. However, unlike the frequent use of *given*, the word *gift* is only used 11 times within the New Testament.[12]

While it is difficult to precisely pinpoint exactly what gift Christ is said to have given, there is textual support to see that the gift Paul is referring to is, in a general sense, grace or possibly, in a specific sense, the Holy Spirit. Regarding the general aspect, all the places this word gift is used, outside of Acts, grace, or salvation is in view. Within the book of Acts, the gift given is specifically the Holy Spirit.

Returning to verse 7, Paul is indicating that distinctions within the body of Christ exist according to the measure or sovereign choice of Christ's gift. This is similar to what Paul said in Romans 12:3 before introducing distinctions within the body. There he writes, "but to

---

9 BDAG, 213.

10 BDAG lists 17 definitions for this word.

11 BDAG, 266.

12 John 4:1; Acts 2:38; Acts 8:20, 10:45, 11:17; Rom. 5:15, 17; 2 Cor. 9:15; Eph. 3:7, 4:7; Heb. 6:4.

think with sober judgement, each according to the measure of faith that God has assigned." In both passages we can see that God and Christ are sovereignly assigning or giving faith and grace to believers.

However, lest we think that Paul is indicating some believers are more saved or less saved because of the measure of faith or grace they have received, we must remind ourselves of the point that Paul has just labored to make in Ephesians 4:1–6 regarding the unity of the body of Christ. "There is one body and one Spirit" (Eph. 4:4). Therefore, some believers are not more saved or less saved than other believers.

Distinctions do exist within the unified body of Christ, and these distinctions have been given by God the Father and Christ, according to their sovereign design. What is more, this is the exact same point that Paul makes in 1 Corinthians 12, where he more fully explains the body metaphor that he employs.

The point is this, the *gift* in verse 7 is not a spiritual gift per se, but rather the general gift of grace or salvation, and possibly the specific gift of the Holy Spirit, whom Christ has given to us as a helper (John 14:16–17). Before distinctions between different spiritual gifts are enumerated, Paul first places tremendous emphasis on the unity of the body and the gift of grace that all believers have received from Christ.

Providing further explanation of Christ's role in specifically gifting his people with spiritual gifts, Paul turns to the Old Testament and quotes Psalm 68:18. In this quotation, Paul repeats his use of the word *gave* and adds a third word (δόμα) that is also translated as *gifts* in our English Bibles, built from the same Greek root word. The word *gifts* (δόμα) simply means *gift* and is only used four times in the New Testament.[13]

In verse 7, the action was the general giving of grace and, perhaps more specifically, the gift of the Holy Spirit. In verse 8, Paul shifts his attention from grace and the Holy Spirit to actual gifts.

Regarding Paul's use of Psalm 68 and Christ's victory "far above every rule and authority and power and dominion ..." (Eph. 1:21) Beale and Carson note, "The Christ who in his descent to earth and

---

13 BDAG, 256. Matthew 7:11; Luke 11:13; Ephesians 4:8; Philippians 4:17.

ascent to heaven triumphed over all his cosmic enemies is the same Christ who from his position of triumph at God's right hand distributes diverse gifts to his people in order to foster their unity."[14]

Paul's point here is to magnify the totality of Christ's victory and the absolute authority with which he now rules and reigns. The King has conquered and now gives gifts to his people. Furthermore, he does so to unite, equip, and build up His body (Eph. 4:12).

Offices or Gifts

In comparison to the other lists of spiritual gifts that Paul gives in 1 Corinthians and Romans, the list found in Ephesians 4 is relatively short. However, brevity is not a synonym for insignificance. In fact, the four or five gifts that Paul lists in Ephesians 4 have tremendous significance for the church.

As we work through the gifts that Paul lists in verse 11, we first need to determine whether Paul is referring to offices or gifts. Interpreting his intent will greatly inform and determine how we see this list coexisting with Paul's other lists. While there certainly are some who interpret all four or five gifts as offices, a majority interpret only Apostle and Prophet as offices and thus conclude that evangelist, shepherd, and teacher are gifts.

Several arguments can be offered in favor of interpreting *apostle* and *prophet* as offices that have ceased and not gifts:

First, Paul uses the words *apostle* and *prophet* in both Ephesians 2 and Ephesians 3, and in both instances the most natural way to interpret his use of these words is to see him referring to the office of Apostle and Prophet. To assert then that Paul uses the words *apostle* and *prophet* one way in Ephesians 2 and 3, and a different way in Ephesians 4 is problematic exegetically.

Second, the consistency with which Paul uses *apostle* throughout his writings would indicate that the office of Apostle would most naturally be in view not a gift.[15] Similar to the first point, to conclude that

---

14 Beale and Carson, *Commentary on the New Testament*, 824.

15 See the arguments made for how I have interpreted *apostle* in 1 Corinthians 12:28–29.

Paul would use these same words and mean something different than the way he has commonly used these terms elsewhere is problematic exegetically.

Third, there is theological coherence in interpreting *apostle* and *prophet* to be offices that have ceased. This coherence emerges as we consider two important truths.

God's call and use of capital "A," Apostles in the New Testament and capital "P," Prophets in the Old Testament; namely, their role in communicating God's word to God's people through the inspiration of the Holy Spirit. The author of Hebrews writes, "Long ago, at many times and in many ways, God spoke to our fathers by the prophets ..." (1:1).

The implications that arise from concluding that the office of Apostle and Prophet still exist today and are operable in today's church are significant and troublesome.

For example, to conclude that the office of Apostle still exists today is to conclude that individuals today still can say and do all the things Apostles in the New Testament did, including receiving new special revelation from the Holy Spirit and performing signs and wonders. Admittedly, it is much cleaner exegetically to conclude that Paul's use of apostle and prophet in Ephesians 4 is an office that has ceased. Such a conclusion retains the uniqueness of the Apostle and Prophets and shuts the door to those unique roles continuing today.

Also, in 1 Corinthians 15:7–8, Paul himself communicates a lack of apostolic succession when he states that he was the last of all the apostles to whom Christ appeared. Again, it is exegetically problematic to conclude that Paul writes in verse 8 that he was the last Apostle and then to conclude from Ephesians 4 that the office of Apostle still endures today.

There is good evidence to support the conclusion that the *apostle* and *prophets* Paul refers to were those who occupied the office of Apostle and Prophet. However, there are also good points of counterevidence which support the conclusion that Paul intends *gifts* to be understood.

To Each Is Given

In support of *gifts,* we need to note that Paul specifically uses the word *gifts* in verse 8 to describe the list in verse 11. As noted above, what is given by Christ in verse 8 is not a general gifting of grace or the specific gifting of the Holy Spirit. It bears repeating, Christ has given gifts to his people, who are his body (Eph. 1:22), to unite, equip, and build up His body (Eph. 4:12).

In his commentary on Ephesians, Harold Hoehner gives six distinctions as to why this is a list of gifts and not offices. His reasons are:

1. The term *office* appears to be limited to apostle (Acts 1:21–25), elders/bishops (1 Tim. 3:1–7; Titus 1:5–11), deacons (Acts 6:1–6, 1 Tim. 3:8–13), and possibly deaconesses (1 Tim. 3:11, Rom, 16:1).[16]

2. Gifts are sovereignly bestowed by God; those holding offices were either appointed or selected based on qualifications.

3. Everyone has a gift, but not everyone has an office.

4. Marital status is mentioned for the offices of elders and deacons, but no such qualification exists for those who are given gifts.

5. Those holding offices cannot be novices. There is no such restriction for those who are given gifts.

6. Certain offices must be held by men, whereas those who have gifts may be either gender.[17]

The other point to consider is the slight grammatical variation Paul uses between chapters 2 and 3 and chapter 4. In chapters 2 and 3, the definite article, *the*, only appears once and refers to Apostle and Prophets. In chapter 4, Paul uses the definite article *the* before each of the gifts he lists except teacher. In fact, the lack of the definite article before teacher is why there is some debate on whether shepherd-teacher is the last gift Paul lists or whether shepherd and teacher are separate gifts within this list. Consequently, while this point of evidence should not be considered definitive by itself, it is instructive and worth considering among all the evidence.

---

16 Emphasis mine.

17 Harold Hoehner, *Ephesians: An Exegetical Commentary* (Grand Rapids: Baker Academic, 2002), 539.

As was noted earlier, this passage in Ephesians 4 does not fit cleanly, exegetically speaking, with the other lists Paul has given and his use of the words *apostles* and *prophets* in chapters 2 and 3. Furthermore, it does not appear that conclusive evidence is available to fully settle the question. As such, we are left with a difficult task in interpreting what Paul intended the Ephesian church to understand.

I believe that Paul is writing about spiritual gifts in Ephesians 4 and not offices. While there certainly are similarities between the offices of Apostle and Prophet and the gifts of apostles and prophets, we do not need to conclude that similarity means equity. This is one of the points made in part one of this book regarding the similarities, yet distinctions, between signs and wonders and spiritual gifts. For example, we see the Apostles healing people and are told in Acts 5:12 that "many signs and wonders were regularly done ... by the hands of the apostles." However, even though there is similarity between *gifts of healings* (1 Cor. 12:9) and what the Apostles were doing in Acts, Hebrews 2:4 indicates that there is a distinction. By arriving at this conclusion several theological questions are answered, though admittedly, not all exegetical or theological questions are resolved.

First, since gifts are in view, and not offices, the need to explain why the first two items listed are unique and separate from the following two or three items on the list is no longer an issue. This is especially helpful since the text gives no indication that a distinction is in view within the list itself.[18] Secondly, and similarly to the first, the need to explain why the first two offices on the list ceased while the following two or three remained is removed.

Thirdly, the gifts of apostle and prophet are not giftings that come with the foundational authority and responsibilities of the Apostles and Prophets. Thus, we are guarded from the conclusion that men and

---

18 This is also the argument made regarding the list of spiritual gifts in 1 Corinthians 12:8–10. One cannot determine from the text alone that Paul intends for the list in 1 Corinthians to be broken up into sub-categories of "sign gifts" and "edifying gifts." This is a theological conclusion, not an exegetical conclusion.

women today may be used by God to reveal new Scripture.[19] Lastly, this conclusion gives us language to explain how God used other individuals in the early church who are cited as apostles and prophets, but who were not called to the office of Apostle and Prophet.[20]

As we seek to understand what Paul has written in Ephesians 4 and its importance for the church today, we must turn our attention next to a very significant question. Can both men and women be gifted with the gifts of Ephesians 4 or are the gifts listed in Ephesians for men only?

---

19 This creates a direct and significant distinction contra Wagner and the NAR.

20 See Philippians 2:25 and 2 Corinthians 8:23 for examples of apostles and Acts 11:27–28 and 21:9–10 for examples of prophet, or those who prophesied.

16
GENDER ROLES AND SPIRITUAL GIFTS

Questions about the role of women in the church are not new. In fact, the relationship between women and men, in life and ministry, has been fraught with dysfunction and disunity ever since the fall in Genesis 3 when God cursed the "very good" (Gen. 1:31) roles that he had given to the man and woman in Genesis 2.

Within the marriage relationship we see that the woman will now accomplish her role as a helper fit for him (Gen. 2:18) in pain (Gen. 3:16). Her natural inclination will now be against her husband (Gen. 3:16).

The man will now, in pain (Gen. 3:17), accomplish his role as initiating leader to tend the garden (Gen. 2:15). Because of the curse, however, he will be naturally inclined to dominate and lord over his wife (Gen. 3:16).

What God had originally designed and declared to be *very good* has now been deeply marred by sin and forever affected until the new heaven and new earth (Rev. 21). Adding to these difficulties are the different ways biblical gender roles have been confused within the American culture and church over the last several hundred years.

Unfortunately, the biblical role of women has been colloquially reduced to being "barefoot, pregnant, and in the kitchen" and most assuredly the laundry room as well. Men, in turn, are the ones who have to "change the oil, balance the checkbook, and fix the leaky faucet in the bathroom." These sarcastic descriptions of where people generally default are a far cry from the complementing-interdependence that God created Adam and Eve to have for and with one another.

To Each Is Given

Functionally problematic to these societal gender roles (which are not biblical) are the questions, "what if he can't add?" and "what if she can't cook?" Must this family persist in having an unbalanced checkbook and burnt meals week in and week out because society, or worse yet, the church, demands that this man and woman occupy these stereotyped roles?

No, the role of headship or initiating leader that God has given to men is to ensure the checkbook is balanced, not to balance the checkbook. Therefore, if he can't add, and she has a degree in accounting, he should not be the one who manages the finances! His role is to make sure the finances are managed according to biblical principles.

The point in briefly considering the *very good* roles that God has given to men and women matters greatly as we think about the gifts in Ephesians 4 and whether these gifts are just for men, just for women, or for both men and women. Likewise, within a local church, God has given the role of initiating headship and responsibility to a plurality of qualified elders. This office—elder/overseer/pastor—is uniquely set apart from the office of deacon and other areas of local church serving by the requirement of teaching, that is only found in the qualifications of elder.[1]

As was noted in chapter 15, the gifts listed in Ephesians 4 are gifts and not offices of ministry that certain individuals occupy. Consequently, as Hoehner points out, there is no list of qualifications that must be met for an individual to be given a certain spiritual gift, and no list of qualifications that must be met for a certain individual to use the spiritual gift they have been given.[2]

Therefore, the gifts listed in Ephesians 4, as in the other passages about spiritual gifts, are for both men and women and given according to the sovereign will and design of our triune God. Women

---

1 More commonly than not, the title Pastor is used to refer to one who occupies a specific, and usually paid, position of leadership within a local church. By and large pastors within the Charis Fellowship are required to meet the qualifications of elder/ overseer that are found in 1 Timothy 3 and Titus 1.

2 cf. paraphrase of Hoehner in the previous chapter.

are gifted by Jesus as apostles, prophets, evangelists, shepherds, and teachers and men must do everything they can not to merely *allow* them to serve, but also to champion their service! Furthermore, it is my conviction that the only office of ministry that is reserved for men is the office of elder/overseer/pastor if we are using the word pastor as is commonly used in our churches today, and not referring to the spiritual gift of shepherding.[3]

A common objection made to the conclusion that these gifts are given to both men and women is Paul's language in Ephesians 4, specifically the gender of each noun. The terms apostles, prophets, evangelists, shepherds, and teachers are masculine, and this leads some to conclude that these gifts are for men only.[4]

Without diving deep into Greek grammar rules, it should be noted that "a word is not always the gender you might expect."[5] Mounce continues, "ἁμαρτωλός means 'sinner' and is masculine, but it does not mean that a sinner is male. ἁμαρτία means 'sin' and is a feminine noun but does not mean that sin is a feminine trait."[6] We cannot simply conclude that these gifts are reserved for men only because the gender of these nouns is masculine. Rather, our interpretations must certainly follow the rules of Greek grammar but also be consistently applied.

For example, to conclude that the gifts in Ephesians 4 are only for men because of the masculine gender of the nouns would mean that we must also conclude that Paul's use of the word *saints* (Eph. 4:12) is only referring to men because its gender is masculine! Such a conclusion would mean that Paul only intends for men within the body of Christ to be equipped and built up.

---

3 A similar argument can be made here about the wisdom of using the term "pastor" as was made regarding calling a church planter an "apostle." To refer to someone who is gifted as a shepherd but does not meet the qualifications of elder/ overseer, pastor is more than likely unhelpful because of how these words are commonly understood and used in our churches today.

4 This interpretation is usually held by those who also conclude that apostle and prophet are *offices*, not *gifts*, that ceased with the completion of the canon.

5 William Mounce, *Basics of Biblical Greek* (Grand Rapids: Zondervan, 2003), 29.

6 Ibid.

To Each Is Given

Furthermore, we would also have to conclude that the gifts in Romans 12 are reserved only for women because each of those nouns is feminine. Nevertheless, I know of no interpreter who believes the gifts in Romans 12 are exclusively for women, or that the equipping of *saints* in Ephesians 4:12 is only for men.

When the list in Ephesians 4 is understood to be gifts and not offices, these questions of gender and gender roles become nonissues. Because there is no formal office directly associated with these gifts, men and women can both receive from Jesus the gifts that He wants them to have, and they are both equally responsible for using the gifts they have been given for His glory and the building up of the body.

One last important note needs to be made regarding these gifts and their exercise. Because gifts and offices are separate, to have a specific gifting does not mean you invariably function within a correlating office. For example, the office of elder requires that the men serving as elders be able to teach (1 Tim.3:2). Some of these men may be gifted as teachers, others may not. The qualification is not that they are *gifted* to teach, but that they are *able* to teach. Conversely, women who are gifted as teachers, for example, do not have to be elders to be great teachers and use the gift that they have been given in ways that follow the biblical guidelines set forth by the New Testament.

Shepherding is another area where women can be gifted, but this gifting does not demand that they function as elders or be called *a pastor*. Furthermore, not all the men serving as elders may have the gift of shepherding even though they are commanded to shepherd by virtue of the office they have called to.[7]

Jesus gives both men and women in His church gifts with which to serve His body. Yes, there is a restriction made regarding gender and the office of elder, but this is the only gender restriction that is made within the local church and does not affect how men and women may be gifted by Christ.

---

7 Acts 20:28, 1 Pet. 5:2

How, then, is the church equipped for ministry and built up for ministry by the persons with these gifts? Next, we turn our attention to defining the entire list of gifts in Ephesians 4.

17

THE GIFTS IN EPHESIANS 4

The five gifts listed by the Apostle Paul in Ephesians 4 are apostle, prophet, evangelist, shepherd, and teacher (or shepherd-teacher). Christ has given each gift to His church for its equipping and building up, and each gift is needed in our churches today. In this chapter we will seek to define these gifts and what their role is within the body of Christ.

Apostles (ἀπόστολος)—The gift of apostle is seen in those who are sent out to proclaim the gospel as authorized messengers.

In defining this gifts it is important to note that while all believers have been entrusted with "the message of reconciliation," and all are commanded to implore all "on behalf of Christ, [to] be reconciled to God" (2 Cor. 5:19–20) some are specifically gifted to do so as church planters and missionaries. This is similar to how all believers are called to serve (Gal. 5:12) and be generous (2 Cor. 8–9), yet some believers are gifted specifically with service and generosity (Rom. 12:7–8).

In his commentary on the book of Ephesians, Tom Julien helpfully writes, "The term means 'sent ones'; today we call them missionaries, and the Lord gives them to plant the Church where it does not exist or where it once existed but since disappeared."[1] Harold Hoehner adds, "Regarding the gift of apostle for today, it would seem that those who

---

1 Tom Julien, *Inherited Wealth. Studies in Ephesians* (Winona Lake: BMH Books, 1976), 83.

have that gift would function similarly to those in the early church by establishing churches in areas not reached by the gospel. Possibly, this would include missionaries who are involved in establishing churches. The danger is to equate this gift with the office."[2]

The terms *church planter* or missionary are far more common than *apostle* is, and the reason for this is simple. The word *apostle* carries baggage with it from those who have falsely claimed to be Apostles with unique spiritual authority within a local church. While we may know some "bad apple" church planters or missionaries, we do not normally bristle at these gifts or titles in the same way as we do apostle.

The church today is greatly served by men and women who have been gifted as apostles, and the church desperately needs them! However, it may be helpful and wise to choose our terms carefully and define them fully and frequently.

To use the term *apostle* and define it as an "authorized messenger of the gospel/missionary/church planter" is not unbiblical, though many individuals in our churches may not default to this definition. When one hears this term, they may naturally think of Peter or Paul and not of a gifted church planter or pioneering missionary.

However, regardless of the terms, church leaders must never stop asking, "Who has God gifted and called from among us to go and take the gospel to new and unreached places and peoples?"!

Prophets (προφήτης)—The gift of prophet, or those who have the gift of prophecy, are those gifted to proclaim and explain God's Word, and at times receive spontaneous insights (regarding the explanation and application of God's Word) from the Holy Spirit.[3] Those with the gift of prophecy are passionately consumed with God's holiness and concerned for his people to pursue holiness themselves.

As we consider this gift, it is crucial that we understand some fundamental differences between those who occupied the office of Prophet and those today who have the New Testament gift of prophe-

---

2 Hoehner, *Ephesians: An Exegetical Com*mentary, 546–547.
3 Cf. Chapter 9.

cy. Because many of these differences were touched on in early chapters, only a brief summary will be provided here.

The New Testament prophet is not revealing any new words of inspired revelation from the Lord. This was a function of the office of Prophet and has ceased with the completion of the Canon. God has revealed His Word to his people, and we do not need to find new or fresh words from God. What we desperately need is to understand the Word that He has already revealed.

For this reason, Agabus can be called a prophet (Acts 21:10) and have his prophecy disobeyed by the Apostle Paul (Acts 21:13–15). Since Agabus is not one who occupies the office of Prophet, Paul is not bound to obey Agabus's prophecy, and Agabus is not bound to complete perfection regarding his prophecy as was required of Old Testament Prophets (Deuteronomy 18:22). Grudem deals with Agabus's two minor inaccuracies within his prophecy and places what Agabus says in the category of a non-authoritative message from the Lord that did not require every detail to be accurate or for obedience to be demanded.[4]

It is my understanding and conviction that prophets in the church today occupy a needed role of proclaiming and explaining God's Word to God's people, with a visionary emphasis on what obedience and disobedience look like. In slight variance to the teachers who also communicate and explain, the emphasis for the prophet is grasping a vision of what obedience and disobedience to God's Word yields. Therein, this gift may be effective and used in any size group or setting because the purpose of this gift is not merely the act of preaching to a crowd. Furthermore, this is why Paul instructs the church in Thessalonica to "not despise prophecies, but test everything; hold what is good" (1 Thess. 5:20–21) and why he gives the church in Corinth instructions about allowing and judging the prophecies made by those in the church (1 Cor. 14:31–33).

Regarding the *spontaneous insights* that a prophet may receive, three specific notes must be made. First, just because something is

4 Grudem, *The Gift of Prophecy*, 77–83.

spontaneous does not make it better or more effective. Inversely, because something was carefully considered and planned does not make it less effective or beneficial in any way.[5]

Secondly, spontaneous insight(s) should be carefully restricted to the explanation and application of God's Word. *Prophecies* of a new job, more money, health, social status, the gender of an unborn child, etc. do not fit the purpose and usefulness of this gift. In fact, abuses such as these have led many to downplay and ignore the gift of prophecy and its purpose within the body of Christ.

Thirdly, as we seek to interpret, explain, and apply the Scriptures any spontaneous insight must be rejected if it contradicts God's Word in any way. We must never allow a *spontaneous* interpretative insight to supersede an interpretative insight that was arrived at through sound hermeneutics.[6] Equally, we must never allow a spontaneous point of application to undermine the plain meaning and an application of a given passage.

Lastly, spontaneous insights may be wrong, and there must never be any claim of infallibility to any such insight. We must never forget that God's Word is infallible, God's people are not! Therefore, those with the spiritual gift of prophecy must make abundantly sure that they steward this gift in a way that brings glory to God and in no way does harm to the body of Christ.

---

5 This axiom can be applied to many different areas of ministry as well. Spontaneous prayers are not better or more genuine prayers. Transcribed sermons are not less passionate or less effective sermons. Sermon series that are planned "as the Spirit leads" are not more effective than ones planned well in advance! For the Spirit is just as capable of leading nine months in advance as he is nine days, or nine hours, in advance. Lastly (though certainly not finally) spontaneous worship songs are not better songs or more worshipful than songs that were thoughtfully written and composed

6 In the event that a spontaneous insight comes while preaching through a passage, and that insight doesn't seem to fit what had previously been considered through the process of hermeneutics, it is best for the one speaking to not share the insight until they have had time to carefully weigh the insight over/against Scripture. Perhaps it is also best for outside council to be sought out for the purpose of discernment regarding the insight. Personally, I know I am far from infallible in my interpretation, logic, and reasoning. I need a sound hermeneutical strategy and godly people in my life to help protect me from mishandling the Word of God.

Evangelists (εὐαγγελιστής)—The gift of evangelist is seen in those who have a Spirit-empowered ability to preach and share the gospel with everyone they meet. This rare word occurs only three times in the New Testament and refers to a "proclaimer of the gospel"[7]

All believers are commanded to go and make disciples (Matt. 28:19–20), which is an action that requires evangelism. However, certain people within the body of Christ have been gifted by Christ to herald the good news of the gospel.

These individuals will often find themselves caring more about who is not in the church on a given Sunday than who is. To this end, there may be points of conflict that arise between the evangelist, shepherd, and teacher with the latter wanting to focus on those who God has already brought in, and the former wanting to focus on finding more people to share the gospel with.

However, rather than finding one another frustrating, these gifted individuals within the church must recognize their need for one another. The shepherd and teacher can patiently remind the evangelist that the Great Commission is not to make *converts* but *disciples*, and the evangelist can likewise remind the shepherds and teachers that people are heading for hell and need to hear the gospel of Jesus Christ.[8]

Shepherds (ποιμήν)—The spiritual gift of shepherd is the supernatural empowering to love, care for, and minister to God's people. This gift, unlike the others, is a vivid word picture that calls to mind David's words in Psalm 23, Jesus's words in John 10, and Peter's words in 1 Peter 5.

Psalm 23 is a striking comparison between an ancient shepherd and God. Here, David describes God providing all he would need (v. 1);

---

7 BDAG, 403.

8 Granted, this is far easier said than done! Often the evangelist (if not the senior leader in a local church) will feel marginalized, as if their desperate pleas for outreach and simple gospel presentations fall on deaf ears. Similarly, the shepherd, and teacher (if not the senior leader in a local church) will feel as if the evangelist doesn't care to make disciples of those within the local church.

making him lie down in green pastures (v.2); leading him to still water (v. 2); restoring his soul (v. 3); and leading him in the paths of righteousness for his name's sake (v. 3); comforting him with His rod and staff (v. 4).

In John 10, Jesus boldly claims that "I am the good shepherd." What David wrote about God Jesus now claims for himself. As the Good Shepherd, Jesus tells his listeners that he "lays down his life for the sheep." (vv. 11, 15); will not leave the sheep (vv. 12–13); knows his own and is known by his own (v. 14); and has "other sheep that are not of this fold" who He will bring in so that "there will be one flock, one shepherd" (v. 16).

Lastly, because of the imminent return of the Chief Shepherd (1 Peter 5:4), Peter exhorts the elders to shepherd the flock of God (1 Peter 5:2). As under-shepherds of the Chief Shepherd they are to take their lead from the Lord and mimic His actions toward the people He has placed under their care.

Like Christ, they are to exercise "oversight, not under compulsion, but willingly, as God would have you; not for shameful gain, but eagerly; not domineering over those in your charge, but being examples to the flock" (vv. 5:2–3).

The spiritual gift of shepherd is the supernatural empowering to love, care for, and minister to God's people. However, this is a gift that Christ gives freely to those in His body and is not to be confused with the staff position of pastor or the office of elder.

To be sure, there is an overlap between the staff position of pastor, the office of elder, and the spiritual gift of shepherding! Furthermore, all three roles may be working simultaneously in some individuals. Nevertheless, one may be gifted by the Spirit of Christ to love, care for, and minister to the body of Christ and not be called a pastor.[9]

---

9 Anecdotally, I know of one such man personally. He is gifted as a shepherd and used to be a pastor/elder in a local church but is no longer serving in those official roles. His gifting as a shepherd (and responsibility to use the gift he has been given) is in no way diminished despite not being a *pastor* or *elder* in a local church any longer. To merely equate the gift of shepherding to the staff position of pastor and office of elder is unhelpful and has significant ramifications for those who have been gifted this way if they are not in those particular roles.

What is more, one may hold a staff position of pastor and the office of elder, and not be *gifted* by Christ as a shepherd. In this instance, this pastor/elder would be called to obey and carry out the biblical duties of elder (and the general duties of a pastor as commonly understood in North America) though it is not his primary gifting.[10]

Christ has given shepherds to his body. While these persons may be called pastors or serve in the office of elder, it is not necessarily so. One does not need a title or an office to exercise a gift and serve the body of Christ!

Teachers (διδάσκαλος)—The last gift that Paul lists in Ephesians 4 is the gift of teachers.[11] The person who has this gift is supernaturally empowered to teach God's word to God's people! They help connect the dots throughout the pages of the Bible and help God's people understand both the big picture and the important details.

Similarly, to the point made regarding shepherds, those gifted as teachers do not have to be elders, but all elders must be able to teach (1 Tim. 3:2). In this regard, all those called to be elders must be able to adequately and correctly explain God's word to those they are called to shepherd. However, some elders may be supernaturally gifted to teach and shepherd in ways that others are not.

Christ has given gifts to those in His body and therefore, has given His body gifted individuals. These gifted persons

1. Seek to take the gospel where it has never been taken,
2. Proclaim God's word and zealously call His people to holiness,
3. Herald the gospel to the lost and call them to repentance,
4. Love, care for, and minister to the saved, and
5. Provide teaching and instruction in God's inspired Word.

---

10 The idea here is similar to that of the spiritual gift of generosity. All believers are called to be generous because Christ has been generous, regardless if they have been gifted this way or not. However, some believers are gifted with generosity.

11 As noted earlier, some take the absence of the definite article before teachers to be an indicator that only 4 categories of gifts are intended by Paul, with the last gift being shepherd-teachers. While this may be a correct interpretation, I have chosen to keep the list at 5 gifts for the following reasons: 1) It is common today to refer to this list as APEST or the Five-Fold Ministry, and 2) Teaching is not synonymous with shepherding, although the two are closely related.

To Each Is Given

As we have seen throughout the last several chapters, Jesus Christ gives people within His body gifts to serve and build His body. In the next chapter, we will examine the purpose for which these and all spiritual gifts have been given to the church.

18

...TO EQUIP

Our triune God intends for the body of Christ to grow through the direct working of those He has gifted and given to His body! Spiritual gifts are not for the benefit of the gifted person(s). Rather, they are given to people, and those persons are given to the body, for a very specific reason.

Think about that for just a moment and consider the massive implications of this truth. All believers have been gifted by the triune God for the growth and maturation of Christ's body. Therefore, if we do not use our gift(s) and give, the whole body suffers; and if we do not humble ourselves and receive, we ourselves suffer. In this sense, all believers both contribute to the body and receive from the body. This is a direct result of the design that God has sovereignly created.

In 1 Corinthians 12 and Ephesians 4, we looked at how, regardless of what part of the body one is, all parts of the body are equal in value. The various roles and gifts that God has given to the body of Christ do not in any way increase or decrease the value of those in the body.

Continuing in verse 12 of Ephesians 4, Paul lists two specific functions that spiritual gifts have and reveals the purpose these gifts are to accomplish. The gifted persons of verse 11 are to equip the saints for the work of ministry and for building up of the body.

Occurring only one time in the New Testament, *equip* (καταρτισμός) is used in non-biblical Greek as a medical term for "setting a bone, or preparing something."[1] It is closely related to the word καταρτίζω,

---

1 BDAG, 526.

which means "to cause to be in a condition to function well" and is used in the Gospels to refer to the mending of nets.[2] The idea here is that the gifts of verse 11 provide the body what is needed so that the body can work and build. Neil Cole writes, "The gifts given to the church come from Jesus. He placed them in the church so that we can be equipped to serve."[3]

An imperfect illustration of this might be a coach who provides his football team with pads, plays, and training so that the players can go and play the game. Similarly, the gifted persons in verse 11 provide the equipment, plans, and training needed so that saints can work and build. However, the work of serving and building will not end in the fourth quarter after time expires. This work continues.

In fact, one may argue that the work will never cease until Christ consummates the new heavens and new earth. Paul himself indicates this in verse 13 when he writes, "until we all attain to the unity of the faith and of the knowledge of the Son of God, to mature manhood, to the measure of the stature of the fullness of Christ." Ministry is a work that we will make progress in, but is nevertheless a work that is never completed this side of eternity. It also is not accomplished by one individual; rather, it is the body that builds itself and is built by itself.[4]

In this sense, God has created a cycle of giving and receiving within the body of Christ that enables the body to serve, building itself up, and grow. To borrow Paul's body metaphor from 1 Corinthians 12, because the ears are not the sum total of the body, God has created other parts (gifted persons and persons with gifts) so that the ears will

2 Ibid.

3 Cole, *Primal Fire,* 27 Kindle.

4 It is also not a work accomplished solely by those we call *pastor(s).* They must never tell the congregation "I'm the paid guy let me do it," and the congregation must never say "you're the paid guy; you do it." There must be a recognition from the paid staff members that the body is to be equipped and freed to serve. Equally, there is to be a recognition from the body that the paid staff members are not the only ones who do ministry.

mutually benefit from the eyes and the eyes from the ears—both for the purpose of growing together!

The goal of the saints serving and building is given in verse 14. There Paul writes, "so that we may no longer be children tossed to and fro by the waves and carried about by every wind of doctrine, by human cunning, by craftiness in deceitful schemes."

The body is served and built for its members to grow in their knowledge of the Lord Jesus Christ. As a result of such growth, the members of the body and the sum of the parts are guarded from false gospels, false worldviews, falsehoods, and demonic schemes (Eph. 6:11).

19

CONCLUSION

Once again, we return to knowledge. God has revealed in His Word knowledge of Himself and His plan to reconcile sinners to Himself through His Son the Lord Jesus Christ. Such knowledge makes one wise for salvation (2 Tim. 3:14–15), equips men and women for the work of ministry (2 Tim. 3:16), and protects them from the ever-changing winds of false doctrine, human cunning, and lying schemes (Eph. 4:14).

However, knowledge of God, His Word, and the Gospel of Jesus Christ will always be attacked by Satan and his demonic host. We see this begin with the serpent's question to Eve in Genesis 3:1, "Did God actually say?" We see this in Matthew 4:5–7, in the temptation of Christ where Satan himself quotes Scripture to Jesus as he tempts Him in the wilderness. Furthermore, we see this in Paul's description of unbelievers in Romans 1:25, who have "exchanged the truth [true knowledge] about God for a lie [false knowledge about God and themselves] and worshipped and served the creature rather than the Creator." Consequently, it should come as no surprise to us that the church today is spiritually attacked regarding truth and knowledge.

Jesus warned His listeners in Matthew 7:15 to "beware of false prophets, who come to you in sheep's clothing." Paul gives the same instructions in many of his letters as he writes to correct errors a church might have believed and/or to warn these churches to be on guard.[1]

---

1 Acts 20:28–30; Romans 16:17–18; 1 Corinthians 5:1–2; 2 Corinthians 11; Galatians 1:9; Ephesians 4:14, 6:11; Philippians 3:2–11; Colossians 2:8, 2:16–19;

TO EACH IS GIVEN

In 2 Timothy 3, as Paul instructs his young protégé regarding the last days, he not only tells him that unbelievers will "always [be] learning and never able to arrive at a knowledge of the truth," but he also instructs him to "continue in what you have learned." Once again, we see truth in the forefront of the battle that rages and how believers are to fight. To borrow Paul's metaphor from Ephesians 6, Timothy is to never take off the belt of truth as he pastors the church in Ephesus.

As I have sought to argue throughout this book, it is *because* truth and knowledge are so important that we must not set aside what the Scriptures teach regarding spiritual gifts. My journey toward continuationism was exclusively informed by the Text, and not my experiences or desires.[2] I believe the Bible gives solid evidence that all spiritual gifts are still active for today.

However, the solidifying of my concerns regarding the hyper-charismatic movement and the NAR have been further deepened by the Text. I believe, more so then ever before, there is significant spiritual danger within these theological movements. Consequently, in desiring to use the gifts the triune God has given to us we must not ever go beyond what God has revealed to us in His Word.

No spiritual gift requires or will lead any believer to set aside what God has clearly revealed in His Word. Or to state it another way, we do not need to set aside knowledge of God's Word in one passage to obey God's Word in another passage. In fact, as Paul makes clear in 2 Timothy 4:3–4, the setting aside of God's Word is a characteristic of false teachers. To this end, we must always be on guard against anyone, or any theological system, that twists what God has revealed or claims that God is revealing new Scripture through them.

---

2 Thessalonians 2:1–12; 1 Timothy 1:3–11, 4:1–3, 6:3–10; 2 Timothy 3:1–9, 4:3–4; Titus, 1:10–11.

2 I fully recognize this is a subjective claim and one that is not easily countered. Nevertheless, as I have labored over this project and spent time preaching through 1 Cor. 12-14, I believe the Scriptures to teach these truths and believe I can stand before the Lord with a clear conscience that I have desired nothing more than to understand His Word, obey it, and teach it to others.

Even though spiritual gifts are an area of theological distortion and doctrinal error, we must work hard at upholding and obeying what God has revealed in His Word. In this way, God intends for His Spirit-filled sons and daughters to be always mind-full in their walk with Him and interaction with others. The church today must fully embrace and use the spiritual gifts that she has been given! As we have seen, these gifts are intended to build up and protect the church, and the church desperately needs all the gifts of the Spirit to be used in the way God intends. Nevertheless, the church must not embrace any use of spiritual gifts that requires or encourages the setting aside of mind-fullness.

We must also take care not to conclude that rational thought is the only goal, or all we need. Indeed, Paul writes in Ephesians 4, that spiritual gifts are to protect correct thinking and to guard from error. However, this does not mean that we will be able to rationally explain everything the Holy Spirit does!

To be sure, the empowerment of spiritual gifts by the Holy Spirit should lead the church to worship as she marvels at the Spirit's work in and through her. However, not being able to rationally explain everything the Holy Spirit empowers does not mean we are called to set aside rational thought as a precursor to the Spirit's working. God is not pleased with, nor does He empower chaos! Rather, He is a God of peace, not confusion (1 Cor. 14:33).

As we seek to use our gifts and build the body as God has designed, we must never forget that if have not love for one another it does not matter what we do (1 Cor. 13:1–3). We must love with a love that sacrifices and surrenders for the good of the body.

To each has been given ... so that each may build and grow in love.

Appendix A

A Specific Reference to Inspired Scripture	A Reference to a Non-Scripture Message
	Matthew 7:22 (v)
Matthew 11:13 (v)	
Matthew 13:14 (n)	
Matthew 15:7 (v)	
	Matthew 26:68 (v)
Mark 7:6 (v)	
	Mark 14:65 (v)
Luke 1:67 (v)	
	Luke 22:64 (v)[1]

---

1 Matthew 26:68, Mark 14:65, and Luke 22:65 all record the same event when Jesus was blindfolded and being struck by the guards. While beating him, the guards mocked Jesus demanding that he "prophesy" and tell them who it was that struck him. I have put these three instances in the non-Scripture category because the guards were not asking Jesus to reveal Scripture to them.

To Each Is Given

A Specific Reference to Inspired Scripture	A Reference to a Non-Scripture Message
John 11:51[2] (v)	
	Acts 2:17 (v)
	Acts 2:18 (v)
	Acts 19:6 (v)
	Acts 21:19 (v)
	Romans 12:6 (n)
	1 Corinthians 11:4 (v)
	1 Corinthians 11:5 (v)
	1 Corinthians 12:10 (n)
	1 Corinthians 13:2 (n)[3]
	1 Corinthians 13:8 (n)

2 Luke 1:67 and John 11:51 are difficult to put neatly into one of these two categories because it is probable that the ones speaking (Zechariah and Caiaphas respectively) did not know they were uttering a message that carried the weight of Scriptural authority. However, Luke and John record what they said, and the Holy Spirit gives their messages this level of authority by including it in the canon.

3 An argument could be made here that since Paul is referring to himself, that this could be a reference regarding Scripture. However, given that in 1 Corinthians 13:1–2 Paul lists 5 of the 8 spiritual gifts he just outlined in chapter 12 it seems best to understand this reference to "prophetic powers" as one not pertaining to the authoring of Scripture.

Appendix B

It is incredibly important for us to have some method for evaluating and determining which leaders, ministries, and resources we will utilize, and learn from, and recommend to others. Below are the criteria that I provided my congregation when preaching through 1 Corinthians 12. It functions as a litmus test for me as I evaluate various sources. The first three points give me pause and lead me to be cautious; the final two are immediate red flags for me.

Do They Use Scripture Like a Conspiracy Theorist Uses Random Facts? I suspect we've all seen it before, whether in a movie, TV drama, or news outlets (unfortunately), random unrelated facts and details are woven together to create a plausible explanation. While this may make for good entertainment, it's a terrible method for interpreting God's Word.

At the heart of this first bullet lies the hermeneutic, or Bible interpretation method, that an individual, ministry, or denomination may employ. In working on this book, I consulted multiple sources and authors within the NAR, for example, and found many of them redefined entire biblical concepts and words to give proof to what they were teaching.

Charis Fellowship Churches have defined their hermeneutic in the *Charis Commitment to Common Identity* (CCCI), and I have written about and explained our hermeneutic as part of a developing project spearheaded by *Inspire: The Charis Pastors Network*. Visit https://

www.inspirepastors.org/documents and click on "Charis Beliefs" for a download of several short papers about a variety of topics. The paper on hermeneutics can be found here and is entitled "hermeneutics (3.2)."

Do They Make Extra-Biblical Demands on My Life? I'm always hesitant when someone makes demands on my life that are not specifically found in Scripture. At issue here would be the pastor's, ministry's, or denomination's understanding of their authority in my life. Where God has specifically commanded in His Word we can and should be clear. Where we believe we know what someone should exactly do (outside of biblical revelation) we should be humble and cautious.

Is the Emphasis Knowledge or Emotion? Admittedly, this is a subjective point of testing and can be driven by personality type. However, as contended above I believe God has chosen to communicate to His people in words, through His Word. As such, He desires for His Word to be understood. Consequently, I am always going to be hesitant and cautious when the emphasis is first on emotion, and secondly propositional truth.

Are There Extra-Biblical Guarantees Made? God makes tremendous promises in His Word and desires His people believe what He has said. However, many of the promises being made by NAR and hyper-charismatic churches and leaders are extra-biblical. Guaranteed healing here on earth, promises of financial increase, prophecies regarding the gender of a child and the increase of fame and/or success are all red flags for me. I do not follow leaders who speak and lead in these ways.

Is Jesus a Means to Another End Rather than the End? The gospel is the good news that God and sinners can be reconciled through the substitutionary death of Jesus Christ. The glory of the gospel, the good news we have been sent out to proclaim, is that we can spend eternity with God! Nothing is greater than that promise.

Consequently, I reject pastors, ministries, and denominations, that seek to make eternal salvation secondary and not primary. To say it another way, they preach and teach that Jesus is a means to another end, not the end himself.

To be sure, a relationship with Christ does, and should, affect every aspect of our lives and we should see major functional changes and differences as we seek to live in obedience to Him. However, Jesus didn't die so that I could merely have good health, or money, or American prosperity. The abundant life that Jesus promises in John 10:10 must not be defined by capitalistic gain, but rather by God Himself in His Word.

Acknowledgments

I have always read the acknowledgments page at the end of books, but never personally understood the tremendous significance of the team it takes to complete a project like this.

The bones of this project began as a position paper that I submitted to the Elder Team at my church. For a few months, I had been sensing the Lord's prompting to preach through 1 Corinthians. Knowing that chapters 12–14 were unavoidable, I submitted this paper to them so that we could discuss what I believe the Scriptures to teach about spiritual gifts well in advance of my actual preaching. Their initial feedback and questions were invaluable to the development of this project, and I am grateful for their willingness to listen, their thoughtful engagement, and their support. Thank you, Joe Beckner III, Kevin Bedell, John Fitz, Danny Hafer, Dwaine Martin, John Poper, and Justin Walter.

Thank you, Thomas Clothier, Dave Ermold, Joyce Fitz, David Fisher, and Jennifer Wagaman for your editing help. You all brought something unique and different to this project and your questions, suggestions, and feedback are gratefully appreciated.

Thank you, John Sloat, for all the coffee and conversation we have had over the years. Your listening ear, pensive nods, and insightful questions were very helpful in those initial months and years. I wish we lived closer and could keep a weekly coffee appointment on the calendar forever.

To Each Is Given

Thank you BMH for deciding to publish this project and thank you Judy Hagey for making my original manuscript much better! The process of turning in term papers was never a pleasant one for me in college, but working with you has been a joy and delight.

Carrie, my love. You were there at the beginning of this journey and have been a supportive rock each step of the way. To say I couldn't have done it without you sounds cliché but is nevertheless true. Thank you for your patience in listening when I tried to verbally process all that I was learning and synthesize it into something understandable. Your love for the Lord and others is infectious, and I love how you both push me and cheer me on to be a better man. You are God's greatest earthly gift to me and my most precious treasure.

Bibliography

Arndt, William, Frederick W. Danker, and Walter Bauer. *A Greek-English Lexicon of the New Testament and Other Early Christian Literature*. Chicago: University of Chicago Press, 2000.

Beale, G.K. and Carson, D.A. *Commentary on the New Testament Use of the Old Testament*. Grand Rapids: Baker Academic, 2007.

Bill Johnson Ministries: Q&A. "Is it Always God's Will to Heal Someone." February 7, 2018 http://bjm.org/qa/is-it-always-gods-will-to-heal-someone/

Bruce, F.F. *The Book of the Acts*. Grand Rapids: Eerdmans Publishing Company, 1997.

————. *The New Century Bible Commentary: I & II Corinthians*. Grand Rapids, Eerdmans 1971.

Carson, D.A. *Showing the Spirit*. Grand Rapids: Baker Book House, 1989.

Challies, Tim. "Why I am Not Continuationist." July 7, 2016. https://www.challies.com/articles/why-i-am-not-continuationist/.

Chapman, David W. *ESV Study Bible*. Wheaton: Crossway Publishing, 2008.

Chronicle. "Diamonds 'Rain' in Church." June 18, 2014. http://www.chronicle.co.zw/diamonds-rain-in-church/.

Ciampa, Roy and Rosner, Brian. *The First Letter to the Corinthians.* Grand Rapids: Eerdmans, 2011.

Cole, Neil. *Primal Fire.* Tyndale Momentum. 2014. Kindle.

Driscoll, Mark. *Doctrine: What Christians Should Believe.* Wheaton: Crossway, 2010.

Fee, Gordon. T*he First Epistle to the Corinthians.* Grand Rapids: Eerdmans, 2014.

Garland, David. *1 Corinthians.* Grand Rapids: Baker Academic, 2003.

Geivett, R. Douglas and Pivec, Holly. *God's Super-Apostles: Encountering the Worldwide Prophets and Apostles Movement.* Wooster: Weaver Publishing, 2014.

Got Questions: Your Questions. Biblical Answers. "What is Continuationism?" n.d. https://www.gotquestions.org/continuationism.html.

Grudem, Wayne, Gaffin, Richard, Saucy, Robert, Storms, Sam, and Oss, Douglas. *Are Miraculous Gifts for Today? 4 Views.* Grand Rapids: Zondervan Publishing, 1996.

Grudem, Wayne. *The Gift of Prophecy.* Wheaton: Crossway, 2000.

———. *Systematic Theology.* Grand Rapids: Zondervan Publishing, 1994.

Heiser, Michael S. and Vincent M. Setterholm. *Glossary of Morpho-Syntactic Database Terminology.* Lexham Press, 2013.

Hirsch, Alan. *5Q.* Columbia: 100 Movements, 2017.

Hoehner, Harold. *Ephesians: An Exegetical Commentary.* Grand Rapids: Baker Academic, 2002.

Jones, Martyn Wendell. "Inside the Popular, Controversial Bethel Church." *Christianity Today,* April 24, 2016. https://www.christianitytoday.com/ct/2016/may/cover-story-inside-popular-controversial-bethel-church.html.

Julien, Tom. *Inherited Wealth. Studies in Ephesians.* Winona Lake: BMH Books, 1976.

Kent, Homer, Jr. *The Epistle to the Hebrews*. Winona Lake: BMH Books 2002.

———. *Studies in Acts: A History of the Early Church*. Winona Lake: BHM Publishing, 1978.

Kittel, Gerhard, Friedrich, Gerhard, and Bromiley, Geoffrey William *Theological Dictionary of the New Testament*. Grand Rapids, MI: W.B. Eerdmans, 1985.

Greek-English Lexicon of the New Testament: Based on Semantic Domains. Johannes P. Louw and Eugene Albert Nida, eds. New York: United Bible Societies, 1996.

MacArthur, John. *1 Corinthians*. Winona Lake: BMH Books 1984. C.F. pg.44 r.2

———. *The MacArthur Bible Commentary*. Nashville: Thomas Nelson, 2005.

McClain, Alva J. *The Greatness of the Kingdom*. Chicago: Moody Press, 1968.

Mohler, Al. *Christ-Centered Exposition Commentary: Exalting Jesus in Hebrews*. Nashville: B&H Publishing 2017. Kindle.

Mounce, William. *Basics of Biblical Greek*. Grand Rapids: Zondervan, 2003.

Murray, John. *The Epistle to the Romans*. Grand Rapids: Eerdmans Publishing, 1993.

O'Brien, Peter. *The Letter to the Ephesians*. England: Apollos, 1999.

Piper, John. "Spoken, Confirmed, Witnessed: A Great Salvation." *Desiring God*. May 5, 1996. https://www.desiringgod.org/messages/spoken-confirmed-witnessed-a-great-salvation.

Schreiner, Thomas. *Romans*. Grand Rapids: Baker Academic, 2003.

Silk, Danny. *Culture of Honor*. Shippensburg: Destiny Image 2009. Kindle.

Smith, Charles. *Tongues in Biblical Perspective*. Winona Lake: BMH, 1976.

To Each Is Given

Smietana, Bob. "The 'Prophets' and 'Apostles' Leading the Quiet Revolution in American Religion." *Christianity Today*, August 3, 2017, https://www.christianitytoday.com/ct/2017/august-web-only/bethel-church-international-house-prayer-prophets-apostles.html.

Stamps, Donald C. *The Full Life Study Bible*. Grand Rapids: Zondervan Publishing, 1992.

Storms, Sam. *Practicing the Power.* Grand Rapids: Zondervan, 2017.

Stott, John. *The Spirit The Church And The World, The Message of Acts*. Downers Grove: InterVarsity Press, 1990.

Wagner, C. Peter. *Apostles and Prophets.* Minneapolis, Chosen. 2000.

Glossary

Administration—one gifted to lead and guide the church

Discerning Spirits—the supernatural ability to distinguish and evaluate between false spirits and the Holy Spirit; between what is true and what is false

Evangelist—one gifted to preach and share the gospel with everyone they meet

Exhortation—one gifted to passionately encourage the body toward obedience and submission to the lordship of Christ. It includes both the call to repent from sin and the encouragement of discouraged believers

Faith—the ability to trust God and remind God's people never to forget who He is and what He has promised even in the most difficult of human circumstances

Generosity—the Holy Spirit-empowered giving and sharing of resources with others

Gift of Apostle—one empowered to take the gospel to where it has never been

Gift of Prophet—one empowered to proclaim and explain God's Word, and at times receive spontaneous insights (regarding the explanation and application of God's Word) from the Holy Spirit

Gift of Teaching—the Holy Spirit-enabled ability to teach. This gift can be given to either men or women, and the use of this gift has nothing to do with the size or makeup of the audience

To Each Is Given

Gifts of Healings—those gifted by the Holy Spirit to heal

Helping—the ability or capacity to assist

Interpretation of Tongues—the ability to interpret a known, spoken language that is unknown to the interpreter

Kinds of Tongues—speaking in a known language that is unknown to the speaker, for the purpose of proclaiming the gospel

Leadership—the Holy Spirit-enabled ability to influence people to follow a recommended course of action

Mercy—the Holy Spirit-enabled ability to show kindness or concern for someone in need

Office of Apostle—witnesses to the life and ministry of Jesus who were specifically commissioned by Christ to be His authorized messengers. This office ceased with the death of the Apostle John

Office of Prophet—those called by God to speak authoritatively for God. This office ceased with the death of John the Baptist

Office of Teacher—those called to and responsible for teaching God's Word and guarding the church from false doctrine. This office is synonymous with the office of Elder and remains in effect today

Prophecy—the ability to proclaim and explain God's Word and at times receive spontaneous insights (regarding the explanation and application of God's Word) from the Holy Spirit

Service—serving as an attendant, aide, or assistant. This word is closely related to the word deacon, and this spiritual gift empowers men and women to serve and help

Shepherds—those gifted to love, care for, and minister to God's people

Sign(s)—miraculous or non-miraculous events that have special meaning

Signs and Wonders—miraculous acts performed by believers to confirm that they spoke authoritatively for God and that their message was true. Signs and wonders will also be used by the Antichrist, false apostles, and false prophets to lead people away from faith in Jesus Christ.

Utterance of Knowledge—the Holy Spirit-empowered ability to learn and study the Scriptures

Utterance of Wisdom—the Holy Spirit-empowered ability to practically apply biblical knowledge

Wonders—transcendent acts that astound. This term never appears in the Scriptures apart from signs

Working of Miracles—the Holy Spirit-empowered ability to call on God to show up and do miraculous things